Student
Grub

by

Jan Arkless

Contents

Contents

1
Getting Started

When my son first went to university, all the cookery books I could find assumed some basic knowledge of cookery techniques, so I decided to write down my own selection of recipes to give to him. This book is the end result!

It is written therefore for the student who is leaving home for the first time and who knows *absolutely nothing* or *very little* about cooking, or meal planning. It explains the simple things that other cookery books expect you to know by instinct, such as how to boil an egg or fry sausages, how to prepare and cook vegetables *and* have them ready to eat at the same time as the main course.

It includes recipes and suggestions for a variety of snacks and main meals (not all cooked in the frying pan or made from mince) but using fish, chicken, beef, lamb and pork. Since I know that many students prefer not to eat meat, many of the recipes I have included have been written with vegetarians in mind. Most of the meals here are quick, easy and economical to make, but there is a 'Sunday Lunch' chapter near the end of the book.

There are just a few recipes for desserts and cakes as you can easily buy biscuits and ready-made or frozen cakes. Remember that yoghurt makes a good, cheap sweet, and that fresh fruit is the best pud you can eat. Also, fresh fruit juice or milk is far better for you than fizzy drinks or alcohol.

Most recipes in other cookery books are geared towards four or six people, but the majority of the recipes here are designed for the single student cooking for him or herself. However, as many students share flats and houses and sometimes also share the cooking, some of the recipes feed two, three or more. Often it is easier to cook larger portions of stews and casseroles as very small helpings tend to dry up during cooking, so, even if you live on your own, why don't you invite a friend to supper and cook enough for two?

AMOUNTS TO USE WHEN COOKING FOR ONE

Pasta, Noodles, Shapes, etc.
1 very generous cup (3 oz/75g) of uncooked pasta.

Potatoes
3–4 (8 oz/225g) according to size.

Rice
½ cup (2–3 oz/50–75g) dry uncooked rice.

Vegetables
See the individual vegetables in Chapter 5.

Oily Fish
1 whole fish (trout, mackerel, herring).

White Fish
6–8 oz (175–225g) fillet of cod, haddock, etc.

Roast Beef
Approximately 6 oz (175g) per person. A joint weighing 2½–3 lb (1–1.5kg) should serve 6–8 helpings; remember you can use cold meat for dinner the next day.

Minced Beef
4–6 oz (100–175g).

Beef Steak
6–8 oz (175–225g) is a fair-sized steak.

Stewing Steak
4–6 oz (100–175g).

Chicken
Allow a 6–8 oz (175–225g) chicken joint (leg or breast) per person. A 2½–3 lb (1–1.5kg) chicken serves 3–4 people.

Lamb or Pork Chops
1 per person.

Lamb Cutlets
1–3 according to size and appetite.

Roast Lamb
Because you are buying meat with a bone in, you need to buy a larger joint to account for the bone. A joint weighing about 2½ lb (1kg) will serve 4 people well.

Roast Pork
Approximately 8 oz (225g) per serving. A boneless joint weighing 2½–3 lb (1–1.5kg) will give 5–6 generous helpings.

Pork or Gammon Steaks
1 per person or 6 oz (175g).

USING THE OVEN

Temperatures are given for both gas and electric ovens. Remember always to heat the oven for a few minutes before cooking food in it, so that the whole of the oven reaches the appropriate temperature.

REHEATING FOOD

One note of warning: be very careful about reheating cooked dishes. If you must do this, always be sure that the food is re-cooked right through, not merely warmed. *Food just reheated can make you extremely ill if not cooked thoroughly, especially pork and chicken – you have been warned!*

FOLLOWING THE RECIPES

I have given 'preparation and cooking' times for the recipes in this book so that, before you start cooking, you will know approximately how much time to set aside for preparing and cooking the meal. Read the recipe right the way through so that you know what it involves.

The ingredients used in each recipe are all readily available and listed in the order they are used in the method. Collect all the specified ingredients *before* you start cooking, otherwise you may find yourself lacking a vital ingredient when you have already prepared half the meal. When the meal is ready, there should be no ingredients left – if there are, you have missed something out!

Measurements

The ingredients are given in both imperial and metric measurements. Follow one type of measurement or the other, but do not combine the two, as the quantities are not exact conversions.

I have used size 2 or 3 eggs in the recipes so you can use whichever you happen to have in stock. Meat, fish and vegetables can be weighed in the shop when you buy them, or will have the weight on the packet. Don't buy more than you need for the recipe; extra bits tend to get left at the back of the cupboard or fridge and wasted. But it is worthwhile buying some goods in the larger size packets – rice, pasta, tomato ketchup, etc. – as they will keep fresh for ages and be on hand when you need them.

In case you don't own kitchen scales many of the measurements are also given in spoonfuls or tea cups (normal drinking size, which approximates to ¼ pint/5 fl oz/ 150ml; it isn't the American measure of a cup). The following measurements may also be helpful:

Butter, margarine or lard, etc.
1 inch cube (2.5cm cube) = 1 oz (25g); it is easy to divide up a new packet and mark it out in squares.

Cheese
1 inch cube (2.5cm cube) = 1 oz (25g) approximately.

Flour, cornflour
1 very heaped tbsp = 1 oz (25g) approximately.

Pasta (shells, bows, etc.)
1 very full cup = 3 oz (75g) approximately.

Rice
½ cup dry uncooked rice = 2 oz (50g) approximately.

Sugar
1 heaped tbsp = 1 oz (25g) approximately.

Sausages
Chipolatas: 8 sausages in an 8 oz (225g) packet.
Thick sausages: 4 sausages in an 8 oz (225g) packet.

Abbreviations
tsp = teaspoon
dsp = dessertspoon
tbsp = tablespoon (serving spoon)
1 spoonful = 1 slightly rounded spoonful

1 level spoonful = 1 flat spoonful
1 cupful   = 1 tea cup (drinking size cup)
                  approximately ¼ pint/5 fl oz/150ml
                  (*not* the American measure)
pt   = pint

USEFUL STORES & KITCHEN EQUIPMENT

Beg or borrow these from home or try to collect them at the beginning of term, then just replace them during the year as necessary.

Beef, chicken and vegetable stock cubes
Coffee (instant)
Coffee (real)
Cooking oil
Cornflour
Curry powder
Dried mixed herbs
Drinking chocolate
Flour
Garlic powder (or paste)
Gravy granules
Horseradish sauce
Mustard
Milk powder (for coffee)
Orange/lemon squash
Pasta
Pepper
Pickle
Rice (long grain)
Salt
Soy sauce
Sugar
Tabasco sauce
Tea bags
Tomato purée (in a jar or tube)
Tomato sauce

12

Vinegar
Worcester sauce

Also
Dish cloth, washing-up liquid, tea towels, pan scrubber, oven
cleaning powder, oven cloth.

Store sugar, rice, flour, pasta, biscuits and cakes in airtight
containers rather than leaving them in open packets on the
shelf. This keeps them fresh and clean for much longer and
protects them from ants and other insects. Try to collect
some storage jars and plastic containers for this purpose.
(Large, empty coffee jars with screw lids, and plastic ice-
cream cartons are ideal.)

Perishable Foods
These don't keep so long but are useful to have as a start.

Bacon
Biscuits
Bread
Butter
Cereals (such as cornflakes)
Cheese
Chocolate spread
Eggs
Fruit juice
Frozen vegetables
Honey
Jam
Margarine
Marmalade
Milk
Peanut butter
Potatoes

Handy Cans for a Quick Meal
Baked beans
Beans with sausages
Chicken in white sauce
Corned beef
Evaporated milk
Frankfurter sausages
Italian tomatoes
Luncheon meat
Minced beef
Rice pudding
Sardines
Soups (also packet soups)
Spaghetti
Spaghetti hoops
Stewed steak
Sweetcorn
Tinned fruit
Tuna fish
Vegetables (peas, carrots, etc.)

Also
Blancmange powders
Instant whip
Jellies
Pot noodles

Useful Kitchen Equipment
Basin (small)
Bottle opener
Casserole pan (thick heavy ones are the best)
Chopping/bread board
Cling film
Cooking foil
Cooking tongs
Dessertspoons
Fish slice

Frying pan
Grater
Kettle
Kitchen paper
Kitchen scissors
Knives: bread knife with serrated edge;
        sharp chopping knife for meat;
        vegetable knife
Measuring jug
Oven-proof dish (pyrex-type): 1 pint/0.5 litre size is big
    enough for one
Plastic storage containers (large ice-cream tubs are useful, to
    store biscuits, cakes, pasta, etc.)
Saucepans: 1 small; 1 or 2 large ones
Storage jars (large empty coffee jars are ideal)
Tablespoons
Teaspoons
Tin opener
Wooden spoon

Handy but not Essential Kitchen Equipment
Baking tin (for meat)
Baking tins (various)
Basin (large) or bowl
Bread bin
Colander
Egg whisk or egg beater
Electric frying pan/multi cooker (very useful if your cooker is
    very small, old or unreliable)
Electric kettle
Foil dishes (these are cheap and last for several bakings;
    useful if you need a tin of a particular shape or size)
Kitchen scales
Liquidiser
Measuring jug (can also be used as a basin)
Mixer or food processor
Potato masher

Saucepans (extra) and/or casserole dishes
Sieve
Toaster

GLOSSARY

Various cooking terms used in the book (some of which may be unfamiliar to you) are explained in this glossary.

Al dente
Refers to pasta that is cooked and feels firm when bitten.

Basting
Spooning fat or butter or meat juices over food that is being roasted (particularly meat and poultry) to keep it moist.

Beating
Mixing food with a wooden spoon or whisk so that the lumps disappear and it becomes smooth.

Binding
Adding eggs, cream or butter to a dry mixture to hold it together.

Blending
Mixing dry ingredients (such as flour) with a little liquid to make a smooth, runny lumpfree mixture.

Boiling
Cooking food in boiling water (i.e. at a temperature of 212°F/ 100°C) with the water bubbling gently.

Boning
Removing the bones from meat, poultry or fish.

Braising
Frying food in a hot fat so that it is browned, and then cooking it slowly in a covered dish with a little liquid and some vegetables.

Casserole
An oven-proof dish with lid; also a slow-cooked stew.

Chilling
Cooling food in a fridge without freezing.

Colander
A perforated metal or plastic basket used for straining food.

Deep-frying
Immersing food in hot fat or oil and frying it.

Dicing
Cutting food into small cubes.

Dot with butter
Cover food with small pieces of butter.

Flaking
Separating fish into flaky pieces.

Frying
Cooking food in oil or fat in a pan (usually a flat frying pan).

Grilling
Cooking food by direct heat under a grill.

Mixing
Combining ingredients by stirring.

Nest (making a)
Arranging food (such as rice or potatoes) around the outside of a plate to make a circular border and putting other food into the middle of this 'nest'.

Poaching
Cooking food in water which is just below boiling point.

Purée
Food that has been passed through a sieve and reduced to pulp (or pulped in a liquidiser or electric mixer).

Roasting
Cooking food in a hot oven.

Sautéing
Frying food quickly in hot, shallow fat, and turning it frequently in the pan so that it browns evenly.

Seasoning
Adding salt, pepper, herbs and/or spices to food.

Simmering
Cooking food in water which is just below boiling point so that only an occasional bubble appears.

Straining
Separating solid food from liquid by draining it through a sieve or colander, e.g. potatoes, peas, etc., that have been cooked in boiling water.

2
Eggs

Eggs are super value, quick to cook and can make a nourishing snack or main meal in minutes.

In view of the publicity over salmonella in eggs, take care about the eggs you buy and store them sensibly and hygienically – eggs have porous shells and should never be stored where they are in contact with uncooked meat or fish, dust or dirt of any kind. They also absorb smells through the shells, so beware if you are buying fresh fruit, washing powder, household cleaners, firelighters, etc., and keep them in separate shopping bags. Heed the advice on fresh eggs given out by the health authorities: only buy eggs from a reputable supplier and *do not serve raw or lightly cooked egg dishes to babies, pregnant women or the elderly unless you're sure that the eggs are free from bacteria.* There are egg substitutes available in the shops (although you may have to search for them) which you may prefer for safety reasons instead of fresh eggs. Don't panic, but do take reasonable care with egg cookery.

BOILED EGG

Use an egg already at room temperature, not one straight from the fridge as otherwise it may crack. Slip it carefully into a small saucepan, cover with warm (not boiling) water and add ½ tsp salt (to seal up any cracks). Bring to the boil, note the time and turn down the heat before the egg starts rattling about in the pan. Simmer gently, timing from when the water begins to boil, using the table below:

Size	Time	Description
Large (sizes 1 or 2)	3 mins.	soft-boiled
Standard (sizes 3 or 4)	2½ mins.	soft-boiled
Large	4 mins.	soft yolk, hard white
Standard	3½ mins.	soft yolk, hard white
Large	10 mins.	hard-boiled
Standard	9 mins.	hard-boiled

SOFT-BOILED
Remove carefully from the pan with a spoon, put into an egg cup and tap the top to crack the shell and stop the egg continuing to cook inside.

HARD-BOILED
Remove the pan from the heat and place under cold, running water to prevent a black ring forming round the yolk. Peel off shell and rinse in cold water to remove any shell still clinging to the egg.

POACHED EGG

Put about 1 in (2.5cm) water into a clean frying pan and bring to the boil. Reduce the heat so that the water is just simmering. Crack the egg carefully into a cup, and slide it into the simmering water. Cook very gently, just simmering in the hot water, for about 3 minutes, until the egg is set to your liking. Lift it out with a slotted spoon or fish slice, being careful not to break the yolk underneath.

FRIED EGG

Heat a small amount of cooking oil, butter or dripping in a frying pan over a moderate heat (not too hot, or the egg white will frazzle). Carefully break the egg into a cup to check that it is not bad, then pour it into the frying pan and fry gently for 2 to 3 minutes. To cook the top of the egg, either baste the egg occasionally by spooning a little of the hot fat over it, or put the lid on the pan and let the heat cook it. You may prefer the egg carefully flipped over when half done to cook on both sides, but be prepared for a broken yolk. Remove the egg from the pan with a fish slice or wide-bladed knife.

SCRAMBLED EGGS

Usually you will want to scramble 2 or more eggs at a time.

Chopped chives are tasty with scrambled eggs. Simply wash them, cut off their roots and chop them.

Beat the egg well with a fork in a basin or large cup. Add salt, pepper and chopped chives. Melt a large knob of butter in a small, preferably thick, saucepan. Turn heat to low, and pour in the beaten egg, stirring all the time, until the egg looks thick and creamy. Do not overcook, as the egg will continue to cook even when removed from the heat. Stir in (if required) 1 to 2 tsp cream or top of the milk, or a small knob of butter (this helps to stop the egg cooking any more).

CHEESY SCRAMBLED EGGS

Add 1 oz (25g) grated or chopped cheese to the beaten eggs, before cooking.

PAN SCRAMBLE

If you are cooking sausages or bacon as well as scrambled eggs, fry the meat first and then cook the eggs in the same hot fat.

PIPERADE
Serves 1

Scrambled eggs plus a bit extra.

Preparation and cooking time: 30 minutes.

1 small onion
Small green pepper
2 tomatoes (fresh or tinned)
1 tbsp oil, or knob of butter (for frying)
Pinch of garlic powder
Salt and pepper
2–3 eggs

Peel and slice the onion. Wash, core and chop the green pepper. Wash and chop the fresh tomatoes or drain the tinned tomatoes and chop roughly. Heat the butter or oil in a saucepan and cook the onion and pepper over a medium heat, stirring well, until soft (about 5 minutes).

Add the chopped tomatoes, garlic, salt, pepper and stir. Put a lid on the pan and continue to cook gently over a low heat, stirring occasionally, for about 15 to 20 minutes, to make a thick saucy mixture.

Break the eggs into a small basin or large cup. Lightly beat them with a fork, then pour them into the vegetable mixture, stirring hard with a wooden spoon, until the eggs are just setting. Pour onto a warm plate, and eat with hot buttered toast or crusty fresh bread rolls.

SAVOURY EGGS

A cheap and tasty variation on the bacon 'n egg theme; makes a good, quick supper.

For a change, cooked sliced sausages or slices of salami can be used instead of bacon.

Preparation and cooking time: 25 minutes.

1 small onion
1 small eating apple
1 rasher of bacon
2 tsp cooking oil or large knob of butter (for frying)
Salt and pepper
¼ tsp sugar
2 eggs

Peel and slice the onion. Wash, core and slice the apple. De-rind the bacon and cut into ½ in (1.25cm) pieces. Heat the oil or butter in a frying pan over a moderate heat. Add the bacon, onion and apple, and fry, stirring occasionally, until soft (about 5 minutes). Stir in the salt, pepper and sugar.

Remove from the heat. Break the eggs into a cup, one at a time, and pour on top of the onion mixture. Cover the pan with a lid, and cook for a further 3 to 5 minutes over a very low heat, until the eggs are as firm as you like them.

CHEESY BAKED EGG

Quite delicious, and so easy to make.

Preparation and cooking time: 20 minutes.

3–4 oz (75–100g) cheese
2 eggs
Salt and pepper
Large knob of butter

Heat the oven (350°F/180°C/Gas Mark 4). Grease an oven-proof dish well with some butter.

Grate the cheese and cover the base of the dish with half of the cheese. Break the eggs, one at a time, into a cup, then slide them carefully on top of the cheese. Season well with the salt and pepper, and cover the eggs completely with the rest of the cheese.

Dot with the butter and bake in the hot oven for about 15 minutes, until the cheese is bubbling and the eggs are just set. Serve at once, with crusty French bread, rolls or crisp toast, or a salad.

EGG NESTS

These can be served plain, or with the addition of grated cheese, to make a very cheap lunch or supper.

Preparation and cooking time: 30 minutes.

2–4 potatoes
Large knob of butter
2 oz (50g) cheese (optional)
Salt and pepper
2 eggs

Peel the potatoes, cut into thick slices and cook in boiling, salted water in a saucepan for 10 to 15 minutes, until soft. Drain and mash with a fork, then beat in the large knob of butter, using a wooden spoon. Grate the cheese, if used, and beat half of it into the potato. Season with the salt and pepper.

1. Egg nest

Grease an oven-proof dish. Spread the potato into this, and make a nest for the eggs. Keep it warm. Boil 1 in (2.5cm) water in a clean frying pan and poach the eggs. If making cheesy eggs, heat the grill. Carefully lift the eggs out of the water when cooked and put them into the potato nest. If making plain eggs serve at once, otherwise cover the eggs with the remainder of the grated cheese and brown for a few moments under the hot grill. Can be served with a fresh tomato or a salad.

SICILIAN EGGS

Serves 1

Saucy tomatoes with eggs and bacon. Serve with hot toast.

Preparation and cooking time: 25 minutes.

2 eggs
1 small onion
Knob of butter
1 small tin (8 oz/230g) tomatoes
Salt and pepper
Pinch of sugar
Pinch of dried herbs
2 rashers of bacon (de-rinded)

Hard boil the eggs for 10 minutes. Cool them in cold, running water. Shell them, rinse clean, slice thickly and arrange in a greased, heat-proof dish.

Peel and slice the onion, and fry it in the butter in a small saucepan over a moderate heat, until soft (about 5 minutes). Add the tomatoes, salt, pepper, sugar and herbs, and cook gently for a further 5 minutes. Heat the grill.

Pour the tomato mixture over the eggs, top with the de-rinded bacon rashers and place under the hot grill until the bacon is cooked.

If you do not have a grill, fry the bacon in the pan with the onions, remove it and keep it hot while the tomatoes are cooking, then top the tomato mixture with the hot, cooked bacon.

EGG, CHEESE AND ONION SAVOURY   *Serves 1*

Cheap and cheerful, eaten with chunks of hot, crusty bread.

Preparation and cooking time: 30 minutes.

2 eggs
1 onion
Knob of butter (for frying)
1 oz (25g) cheese

For the cheese sauce (you can omit this and just use grated cheese or alternatively use packet sauce mix):
1 oz (25g) cheese
2 tsp flour (or cornflour)
1 cup (¼ pt/150ml) milk
½ oz (12g) butter
Salt and pepper
Pinch of mustard

Hard boil the eggs for 10 minutes. Peel and slice the onion and fry gently in the knob of butter in a small saucepan over a moderate heat, for 4 to 5 minutes, until soft and cooked. Grate the cheese.

For the cheese sauce: EITHER mix the flour or cornflour into a smooth paste with a little of the milk in a small basin. Boil the rest of the milk and pour onto the flour mixture, stirring all the time. Then pour the whole mixture back into the saucepan and stir over the heat until the mixture thickens. Stir in the butter and beat well. Add the 1 oz (25g) grated cheese, salt, pepper and mustard. OR make up the packet sauce mix.

Put the onion into a greased oven-proof dish. Slice the cold, peeled hard-boiled eggs, and arrange on top of the onion. Cover with the cheese sauce and sprinkle with the rest of the grated cheese. Brown under a hot grill for a few minutes, until the cheese is melted, crisp and bubbly.

MURPHY'S EGGS

Serves 1

A cheap and filling supper dish if you have time to wait for it to cook in the oven.

Preparation and cooking time: 1 hour 15 minutes.

½ lb (225g) potatoes (about 3 or 4 according to appetite)
1 onion
1 rasher of bacon
Salt and pepper
½–1 cup (¼ pt/150ml approx.) hot milk
Knob of butter
2 eggs

Peel the potatoes, cut into small ½ in (1.25cm) dice. Peel and slice the onion. De-rind and chop the bacon. Grease an oven-proof dish. Mix the potatoes, onion and bacon in a bowl, and put into the dish, seasoning well with the salt and pepper. Add the hot milk (enough to come halfway up the dish) and dot with the butter.

Bake in a hot oven (400°F/200°C/Gas Mark 6), covered with a lid or foil, for 45 minutes to 1 hour, until the potatoes are cooked and all the milk is absorbed.

Break each egg into a cup. Remove the dish of potatoes from the oven, make two hollows in the top of the potatoes with a spoon, and slip the raw eggs into the hollows. Return the dish to the oven for 6 to 8 minutes until the eggs are set. Serve at once.

EGGY BREAD OR FRENCH TOAST
Serves 1

A boarding school favourite.

Serve with golden syrup, honey or jam, or sprinkled with white or brown sugar.

Or to make it savoury, sprinkle with salt, pepper, and a blob of tomato sauce. Savoury eggy bread goes well with bacon, sausages and baked beans.

Preparation and cooking time: 15 minutes.

1 egg
1–2 tsp sugar (according to taste)
½ cup milk
3–4 thick slices of white bread
2 oz (50g) butter (for frying)

Break the egg into a basin or a large cup, add the sugar and beat well with a whisk, mixer or fork, gradually adding the milk. Pour this egg mixture into a shallow dish or soup plate, and soak each slice of bread in the egg, until it is all soaked up.

Heat a frying pan over a moderate heat. Melt the butter in the pan and fry the soaked bread slices in the hot butter, turning to cook both sides, until golden brown and crispy. Serve at once as above.

FRENCH OMELETTE · *Serves 1*

The best-known type of omelette: light golden egg, folded over into an envelope shape. Served plain or with a wide variety of sweet or savoury fillings, folded inside. There is no need for a special omelette pan (unless you happen to own one, of course). Use any clean, ordinary frying pan.

Preparation and cooking time: 10 minutes.

2–3 eggs
1 tsp cold water per egg
Pinch of salt and pepper (omit for sweet omelettes)
Knob of butter
Filling as required (see opposite)

Prepare the filling (see list opposite). Warm a plate. Break the eggs into a basin or large cup, add the water, salt and pepper and beat with a fork.

Put the butter in a frying pan and heat over a moderate heat until it is just sizzling (but not brown). Place the egg mixture in the pan at once. Carefully, with a wide-bladed knife or wooden spoon, draw the mixture from the middle to the sides of the pan, so that the uncooked egg in the middle can run onto the hot pan and set. Continue until all the egg is very lightly cooked underneath and the top is still running and soft (about one minute). The top will cook in its own heat, when it is folded over.

With the wide-bladed knife or a fish slice loosen the omelette so that you can remove it easily from the pan. Put the filling across the middle of the omelette and fold both sides over it to make an envelope. If using a cold filling, cook for a further minute. Remove from the pan and place on the warm plate. Serve at once, with French bread, bread rolls, sauté or new potatoes, a side salad or just a fresh tomato. Delicious!

OMELETTE AND PANCAKE FILLINGS
For pancakes, see page 241.

Savoury
Asparagus
Use ½ small can (10 oz/298g size) asparagus tips. Heat them through in a small saucepan. Drain and keep hot.

Bacon
Fry 1–2 rashers of bacon in a little oil or fat. Keep hot.

Cheese
1–2 oz (25–50g) grated or finely cubed.

Chicken
2–3 tbsp chopped, cooked chicken. (You can use the pickings from a roast chicken.)

Fresh or Dried Herbs
Add 1 tsp chopped herbs to the beaten eggs, water and seasoning.

Cooked Meat
Chop 1–2 slices cooked ham, salami or garlic sausage, etc.

Mushrooms
Wash and chop 2 oz (50g or 4–5 mushrooms). Cook gently in a small pan, with a knob of butter, for 2–3 minutes, stirring occasionally. Keep hot.

Tomato
Wash 1–2 tomatoes, slice and fry them in a little oil or fat and keep hot.

Sweet
Choose one of the following fillings, then sprinkle the omelettes with 1 tsp icing or granulated sugar, just before serving.

Fruit
Add 2–3 tbsp sliced, tinned fruit (peaches, pineapple or apricot) or 2–3 tbsp sliced fresh fruit (bananas, peaches, strawberries or raspberries).

Honey
Add 2–3 tbsp honey.

Honey and Walnut
Use 2–3 tbsp honey, 1 tbsp chopped walnuts.

Jam
Add 1–2 tbsp jam or bramble jelly. Warm the jam by standing it in a saucepan with 2 in (5cm) hot water, and warming gently over a low heat.

Marmalade
Add 2–3 tbsp orange or ginger marmalade.

SPANISH OMELETTE
Serves 1

A delicious, filling, savoury omelette. Served flat like a thick pancake, mixed with onion, potato, cooked meat and other vegetables – a good way of using up cold, cooked, leftovers. (A large omelette, made with 4 eggs and some extra vegetables, can be cut in half, serving 2 people.)

Preparation and cooking time: 15 minutes.

EXTRAS (optional):

Bacon: 1–2 rashers of bacon, chopped and fried with the onion

Cooked meat: 1–2 slices of chopped, cooked ham, salami, or garlic sausage, etc.

Green peppers: 1–2 tbsp green peppers, chopped and mixed with the onion

Sausages: 1–2 cold, cooked sausages, sliced

Vegetables: 1–2 tbsp cold cooked vegetables (peas, sweetcorn, green beans, mixed vegetables)

1 small onion
2–3 boiled potatoes
2–3 eggs
1 tsp cold water per egg
Salt and pepper
Pinch of dried herbs (optional)
1 tbsp oil (for frying)

Prepare the 'extras' if used. Peel and chop the onion. Dice the cooked potatoes. Beat the eggs, water, seasoning and herbs lightly with a fork in a small basin.

Heat the oil in an omelette or frying pan over a medium heat, and fry the onion for 3 to 5 minutes, until soft. Add the diced potato and continue frying until the potato is thoroughly heated. Add the extra meat or vegetables (if used) and heat through again. Heat the grill and warm a plate. Pour the beaten egg mixture into the pan, over the vegetables, and cook without stirring until the bottom is firm, but with the top remaining creamy and moist (about 1 to 2 minutes). Shake the pan occasionally to prevent sticking.

Place under the hot grill for ½ minute, until the top is set – beware in case the pan handle gets hot. Slide the omelette flat onto the warm plate and serve at once.

QUICK EGG AND VEGETABLE CURRY

Serves 1

A fast and easy curry recipe.

Preparation and cooking time: 35 minutes.

1 onion
Knob of butter
1 tsp cooking oil
1 tsp curry powder (or more or less according to taste)
1 tsp flour or cornflour
Small can (10 oz/295g) mulligatawny soup
2 eggs
½ cup (2–3 oz/50-75g) long grain rice
1 cup or 2 oz (50g) frozen mixed vegetables

Peel and chop the onion, and fry in the oil and butter in a saucepan over a medium heat, until soft (about 3 to 4 minutes). Stir in the curry powder and flour, and cook very gently for a further 2 minutes, stirring all the time. Gradually stir in the soup, bring to the boil, reduce the heat to a simmer, put on the lid, and cook gently for about 20 minutes, stirring occasionally, to make a thick sauce.

Hard boil the eggs for 10 minutes. Rinse them under cold, running water, peel them, wash off the shell and cut in half, lengthways. Cook the rice for 10 to 12 minutes in a large pan of boiling salted water (see page 118). Drain and keep hot, fluffing with a fork to stop it going lumpy. Add the mixed vegetables to the curry sauce, bring back to the boil and simmer for a few minutes to cook the vegetables.

Put the rice onto a warm plate, spreading round with a spoon to form a ring. Arrange the eggs in the centre and cover with the vegetable curry sauce. Serve with any side dishes you like (see page 175).

EGG MAYONNAISE

Make as a starter or a main course.

For each person allow 1 egg as a starter or 2 as a main course.

Hard boil the required number of eggs (simmer for 10 minutes in salted water, cool in cold running water), peel and rinse the eggs to get rid of all the bits of shell.

Arrange a bed of washed shredded lettuce on a large serving dish or individual plates, slice the eggs in rings or cut in half lengthways, and arrange on the lettuce, cut-side-down if halved. Coat the eggs with mayonnaise and garnish with cucumber, tomatoes, green or red pepper strips, cress, watercress, etc., as available. Sprinkle a little paprika, snipped parsley or chives on top of the mayonnaise and serve with brown or granary bread or rolls and butter.

HAM AND EGG PIE   *Serves 3–4*

A useful meal which uses up odds and ends left in the fridge and makes a little meat go a long way. You can use bacon instead of ham if you wish.

Preparation and cooking time: 50 minutes (ham and egg)
60 minutes (bacon and egg).

8 oz (250g) shortcrust pastry – bought or homemade (see following recipe)
4 oz (100g) ham or 3–4 rashers of bacon
2–3 tomatoes, sliced and/or 3–4 oz (75–100g) mushrooms
3–4 eggs – I allow 1 for each person
1 tsp mixed herbs
Salt and pepper
Milk (for brushing)

Heat the oven to 400°F/200°C/Gas Mark 6–7.

Roll out two-thirds of the pastry and line a 7–8 in (18–20cm) sandwich or flan tin. Cut excess fat and rind off the ham or bacon, cut into large pieces and spread over the pastry base. Cover with the sliced tomatoes and/or mushrooms (wash and slice large ones, wash button mushrooms and leave whole). Break the eggs, one at a time, into a cup and slide into the pie, or beat them together and pour over the pie filling. Season with herbs, salt and pepper. Roll out the remaining pastry and cover the pie with a pastry lid, pinching the edges together well. Roll out the remaining scraps of pastry, cut into leaves and decorate the top of the pie.

Brush the pastry with milk and bake the pie in the hot oven for 10–15 minutes until the pastry is lightly coloured, then reduce the heat to 350°F/180°C/Gas Mark 4–5 for a further 15–20 minutes if you used ham, or 25–30 minutes if you used raw bacon rashers.

Serve hot with vegetables or cold with salad, or put a slice in a lunch box as part of a packed meal. Large pies, made with the scrappy pieces of streaky bacon rashers which are often sold very cheaply, make a most economical party buffet dish, served with French bread and big bowls of crisp salads.

SHORTCRUST PASTRY

You'll probably buy frozen pastry if you need to use some, but if you want to make your own, here's a recipe.

Preparation and cooking time: 10 minutes.

To make ½ lb (250g) shortcrust pastry (you measure pastry by the amount of flour used in the recipe):

½ lb (250g) plain flour (self-raising flour gives a puddingy result), plus a little extra flour for rolling out
¼ tsp salt
4 oz (125g) butter, margarine, lard or vegetable fat (I prefer to use a half and half mixture of butter and white fat, butter for colour and flavour, white fat for texture; if you are a vegetarian you won't want to use lard)
8 tsp (approx.) cold water

Sieve the flour and salt into a bowl. Add the chosen fat cut into small pieces. Using the tips of your fingers, rub in the flour and fat to form 'breadcrumbs'. Add the cold water gradually, mixing in with a knife and then using your fingertips to form it into a lump of dough – don't get the pastry too wet (add a little extra flour if it's too sticky) and handle it as little as possible to get a lovely light pastry when cooked. The pastry is now ready to roll out on a lightly floured worktop. It can be wrapped in cling film and left in the fridge until needed.

QUICHE LORRAINE

This is delicious, and uses up any odd bits and pieces you may have left in the fridge! Make a large quiche in a flan dish or ring, or make individual quiches in patty tins – these little ones are nice for a starter, as part of a buffet supper, a packed lunch or a picnic. Use up that one rasher of bacon, the scrappy bits of cheese or the pickings from chicken, turkey or a piece of ham.

Preparation and cooking time: 1¼–1½ hours (large quiche)
55–60 minutes (small ones)

8 oz (250g) shortcrust pastry (bought or made using the previous recipe)

Filling:
1–2 onions
2–3 rashers of bacon (optional)
1 tbsp vegetable oil
2–4 oz (50–100g) cooked chicken, turkey or ham (optional)
2–4 oz (50–100g) Cheddar cheese
2 eggs
½ pint (300ml) milk, pouring cream or a mixture
Salt and black pepper
Pinch of mustard
1 heaped tbsp Parmesan cheese

Heat the oven to 375°F/190°C/Gas Mark 5–6.

Large Quiche
Roll out the chosen pastry and line a 7–8 in (17–20cm) flan dish with it. Prick the pastry all over with a fork and cover the flan with a piece of cooking foil, pressed gently into the flan shape. Bake in the pre-heated oven for about 10 minutes, until the pastry is just set. Remove the foil and return the flan to the oven for 5 minutes, until it is crisp but still pale. Remove it from the oven.

Make the filling: Peel and finely chop the onions and chop the bacon (if used). Heat the oil in a pan over a moderate heat and fry the onion and bacon for 3 to 4 minutes, until the onion is soft and the bacon is nearly cooked. Spoon them into the flan case and cover with the diced chicken, turkey or ham if used, and sprinkle with the grated Cheddar cheese.

Break the eggs into a basin and beat them well with a fork. Mix in the milk and/or cream, season well with salt, pepper and mustard and pour the mixture over the filling in the flan case. Sprinkle with the grated Parmesan cheese.

Bake in the hot oven for 40 to 45 minutes, until it is well risen and golden. If the pastry is getting too brown after 20 minutes, reduce the oven heat to 350°F/180°C/Gas Mark 4–5. Serve hot or cold.

Small Tartlets

Roll out the chosen pastry, cut into 4 in (10cm) rounds, and line 12 patty tins (there's no need to pre-bake these little cases). Prepare the filling as above and divide it between the prepared cases. Bake in the hot oven for 20–25 minutes until risen and golden. Serve hot or cold.

DRINKING EGG OR EGG NOG   *Serves 1*

A nourishing breakfast for those in a hurry, or an easily-digested meal for those feeling fragile!

Preparation time: 5 minutes.

1 egg
2 tsp sugar
2 cups (½ pt/300ml) milk (cold or warm)
2 tsp brandy, rum or whisky (optional, but not for breakfast!)
   or 1 tbsp sherry (optional, but not for breakfast!)
Pinch of nutmeg or cinnamon

Break the egg into a basin, beat it lightly with a mixer, egg whisk or fork, adding the sugar and gradually beating in the milk. Add the spirits (if used). Pour into a tall glass, sprinkle nutmeg or cinnamon on top and serve at once.

HOW TO SEPARATE AN EGG

METHOD 1

Have 2 cups or basins ready. Crack the egg carefully, and pull the 2 halves apart, letting the white drain into one basin, and keeping the yolk in the shell, until all the white has drained out. Tip the yolk into the other basin. If the yolk breaks, tip the whole lot into another basin and start again with another egg.

METHOD 2

Carefully break the egg and tip it onto a saucer, making sure the yolk is not broken. Place a glass over the yolk, and gently tip the white into a basin, keeping the yolk on the saucer with the glass.

3

Cheese

Here are some delicious snacks using cheese – they're simple and quick to make.

EASY WELSH RAREBIT (CHEESE ON TOAST)

Serves 1

This is the quickest method of making cheese on toast. It can be served plain, or topped with pickle, sliced tomato or crispy, cooked bacon.

Preparation and cooking time: 5–10 minutes.

1–3 rashers of bacon (optional)
1–2 tomatoes (optional)
2–3 oz (50–75g/2–3 slices) cheese   *(continued overleaf)*

(Easy Welsh Rarebit continued)
2–3 slices of bread (white or brown)
Butter (for spreading)
1 tbsp pickle (optional)

Heat the grill. Lightly grill the bacon, if used. Slice the tomatoes, if used. Slice the cheese, making enough slices to cover the pieces of bread. Toast the bread lightly on both sides and spread one side with the butter. Arrange the slices of cheese on the buttered side of the toast and put under the grill for 1 to 2 minutes, until the cheese begins to bubble. Top with the tomato slices, bacon or pickle and return to the grill for another minute, to heat the topping and brown the cheese. Eat at once.

TRADITIONAL WELSH RAREBIT *Serves 1*

More soft and creamy than cheese on toast, and only takes a few more minutes to prepare.

Preparation and cooking time: 10 minutes.

1–3 rashers of bacon (optional)
1–2 tomatoes (optional)
2–3 oz (50–75g) cheese
1 tsp milk
Pinch of mustard
Shake of pepper
1 tbsp pickle (optional)
2–3 slices of bread, and butter

Heat the grill. Lightly grill the bacon, if used. Slice the tomatoes, if used. Grate the cheese and mix into a stiff paste with the milk in a bowl, stirring in the mustard and pepper. Lightly toast the bread, and spread one side with butter, then generously cover it with the cheese mixture. Put under the hot grill for 1 to 2 minutes, until the cheese starts to bubble. Top with the bacon, tomato slices or pickle, and return to the grill for another minute, to heat the topping and brown the cheese. Serve at once.

BUCK RAREBIT

Serves 1

Welsh Rarebit with poached eggs. When the toast is covered with the cheese, and ready to pop back under the grill to brown, prepare 1 or 2 poached eggs, by cooking them gently in simmering water for 2 to 3 minutes. While the eggs are cooking, put the toast and cheese slices under the grill to brown. When they are golden and bubbling, and the eggs are cooked, carefully remove the eggs from the water, and slide them onto the hot cheesy toast. Serve immediately.

BOOZY WELSH RAREBIT

Serves 1

Open a can of beer, use a little in the cooking, and drink the rest with your meal.

Preparation and cooking time: 10–15 minutes.

2–3 oz (50–75g) cheese
Knob of butter
1–2 tbsp beer
Shake of pepper
Pinch of mustard
1–2 slices of bread (white or brown)

Grate the cheese and heat the grill. Melt the butter in a small saucepan over a moderate heat. Add the cheese, beer, pepper and mustard, and stir well over the heat, until the cheese begins to melt, and the mixture begins to boil. Remove the saucepan from the heat. Toast the bread lightly on both sides. Carefully pour the cheese mixture onto the toast, and put back under the grill for a few moments, until the cheese is hot, bubbling and golden brown. Serve at once, delicious!

CHEESY FRANKFURTER TOASTS

Serves 1

A quick snack, made with food from the store cupboard.

Preparation and cooking time: 15 minutes.

2–3 slices of bread
½ oz (12g) butter
2–3 slices of cooked ham, garlic sausage or luncheon meat
  (optional)
Small can (8 oz/227g; actual weight of sausages 4 oz/163g)
  Frankfurter sausages
2–3 slices of cheese (pre-packed slices are ideal)

Heat the grill. Lightly toast the bread on one side. Butter the untoasted side of the bread. Lay the ham or garlic sausage on the untoasted side and top with the Frankfurters. Cover with the cheese slices, and cook under the hot grill until the cheese has melted. Eat at once.

If you don't have a grill the bread can be heated in a hot oven (400°F/200°C/Gas Mark 6) for a few minutes, and then buttered. Place the 'toast' with the topping back into the oven, on an oven-proof dish, and cook for 5 to 10 minutes, until the cheese has melted.

PEAR AND CHEESE TOAST

Serves 1

A delicious snack or starter. Use whatever cheese pleases your taste; Cheddar, Edam, Lancashire, Caerphilly or Stilton are lovely.

Preparation and cooking time: 10 minutes.

1 ripe eating pear
1–2 oz (25–50g) cheese
1–2 slices of bread (granary is delicious)
Little butter (for spreading)

Peel and core the pear, and cut into thin slices. Slice the cheese thinly. Toast the bread lightly on both sides under the grill and spread with butter. Arrange the pear slices on the toast, and top with the slices of the cheese. Put back under the hot grill for a few minutes, until the cheese is golden and melted. Serve at once.

CAULIFLOWER CHEESE

Serves 1

Filling enough for a supper dish with crusty French bread and butter, or serve as a vegetable dish with meat or fish.

Preparation and cooking time: 30 minutes.

1 portion (3–4 florets) cauliflower
1 slice of bread (crumbled or grated into crumbs)
Knob of butter
1 sliced tomato (optional)

For the cheese sauce (alternatively use packet sauce mix or 2 oz/50g grated cheese):
2 oz (50g) cheese
2 tsp cornflour or flour
1 cup (¼ pt/150ml) milk
½ oz (12g) butter or margarine
Salt and pepper
Pinch of mustard

Trim the cauliflower's stalk, divide it into florets and wash thoroughly. Cook it in boiling, salted water for 5 minutes, until just tender. Drain well.

Make the cheese sauce (see page 231).

Put the cauliflower into a greased oven-proof dish. Cover with the cheese sauce, sprinkle the breadcrumbs on top and add a knob of butter and the tomato slices. Place under a hot grill for a few minutes, until golden-brown and crispy. (If you do not have time to make the cheese sauce, cover the cauliflower with 2 oz (50g) grated cheese and grill as above.)

CHEESE DIPS AND SPREADS

Feel really virtuous and use up the odds and ends of cheese that seem to accumulate in the fridge, by making them into a dip or a spread, to use at once or freeze for future use if you have access to a freezer. The quantities given in the recipes are approximate – use up whatever amounts you have available.

To produce a stiffer spread to use in sandwiches, omit the liquid.

CHEDDAR CHEESE DIP

2 oz (50g) Cheddar cheese (or any hard-type cheese)
1 oz (25g) butter
2–3 tbsp milk, white wine or cider
Few drops of Worcester or tabasco sauce
Salt and black pepper
Shake of cayenne or paprika pepper

Grate the cheese. Put the butter into a basin and beat until soft, gradually beating in the cheese, and mix to a 'dip' consistency with the milk, wine or cider. Season to taste and pile into a small serving dish. Garnish with a shake of cayenne or paprika and serve with crudités, crisps, savoury biscuits or cheese straws.

BLUE CHEESE DIP

2 oz (50g) butter
4 oz (100g) blue cheese (Stilton, Danish Blue, Gorgonzola, etc.)
2–3 tbsp milk, wine, cider or dry sherry
Salt and black pepper
1–2 tbsp chopped walnuts (optional)

Beat the butter until soft and creamy, crumble in the blue cheese and beat it gradually into the butter, adding enough liquid to make a soft dip. Season with salt and pepper, stir in walnuts if used and heap into a small serving dish. Serve with crudités, or cheese straws, or spoon it onto 2 in (5cm) lengths of washed celery to make party 'nibbles'.

CREAM CHEESE DIP

4 oz (100g) cream cheese or Cambozola
1 oz (25g) butter
Handful of fresh parsley or chives
Few spring onions, very finely chopped
1 or 2 tsp milk, wine or cider

Beat the cream cheese and butter until soft. Beat in the washed snipped herbs and the spring onions, adding a few drops of liquid if the mixture is too stiff. Pile into a serving dish and serve with crudités, crisps or biscuits as above.

ANNABEL'S CHEESE FONDUE

Serves 2

You don't need a special occasion to enjoy a fondue. This is one of my daughter's favourite recipes. It makes a nice cosy supper for two in the winter, or is equally good for a leisurely light lunch in the summer – you can even eat it outside on a hot, still day. It's a good way of using up odds and ends of cheese to make a cheap meal.

Fondue is easiest to make in a proper fondue pot with a burner underneath to keep it warm, but cheese fondue will work very well made in a small, thick saucepan without a burner, as it does not need to be kept boiling like an oil fondue; put it on a hotplate if you have one. The fondue will reheat over a very, very low heat if necessary, and you can use forks instead of fondue sticks.

Preparation and cooking time: 20 minutes.

1 French stick or 4–5 fresh bread rolls
1 clove of fresh garlic
8 oz (225g) cheese – a mixture of Gruyère and Emmental is traditional, but you can substitute the much cheaper Cheddar, Edam or whatever cheese you have left over
2 tsp cornflour or flour
1 cup (¼ pt/150ml) dry white wine or cider (or use non-alcoholic wine or apple juice if you prefer)
1 tsp lemon juice
1 tsp herb or whole grain mustard
Plenty of black pepper

Cut the bread into large bite-sized chunks and put in a serving dish. Peel the garlic, cut it in half and crush or rub it well around the base and sides of the fondue pot, to leave a good garlicky flavour. Discard the garlic pieces.

Grate the cheeses. Put the cornflour or flour into a cup and mix to a smooth paste with 2–3 tbsp of the chosen wine, cider or apple juice. Put the remaining liquid into the fondue pot, add the lemon juice and heat gently over a low heat, gradually stirring in the grated cheese and mustard with a wooden spoon, stirring until all the cheese has melted. Remove from the heat, stir the cornflour mixture again, then mix it into the fondue. Return the pot to the heat and cook the fondue, stirring all the time until it is thick, smooth and just bubbling – the heat must remain turned down low all the time.

Season well with black pepper and carefully carry the fondue pot to the serving table and place over a burner if you have one, or on a hotplate or thick table mat. *Always use the correct fuel recommended for your burner (generally methylated spirit) and put the burner in place before lighting. Never carry a lighted burner from kitchen to table.*

Eat the fondue at once, spearing the bread cubes and dipping them into the hot cheese – it's a more filling meal than you might expect. My family like fondue served with a few crudités (sticks of cucumber, carrot, celery, pepper strips, cauliflower florets, radishes, sliced mushrooms, etc.) or a crunchy salad, to off-set the richness of the cheese. A bottle of dry white wine makes a good accompaniment too!

4
Snacks, Savouries and Salads

Just a few ideas and suggestions for quick snacks and packed lunches. Other recipes can be found in Chapters 2 and 3.

SANDWICHES FOR PACKED LUNCHES
Try and ring the changes with different kinds of bread – white, brown, granary, sliced, crusty rolls, soft baps, French bread and Arab bread are a few suggestions. Crisp breads make a change too.

Butter the bread lightly, this stops it going soggy if the

filling is moist, and holds the filling in place (have you ever tried eating unbuttered egg sandwiches?). Wrap the sandwiches in cling film to keep them fresh – it's worth buying a roll if you take sandwiches often – or put them into a polythene bag. A plastic container will stop them getting squashed.

Lettuce, tomato, cucumber, celery and green peppers are a good addition, either sliced in the sandwiches or eaten separately, with them. Treat yourself to some fresh fruit as well, according to what is in season.

Cheese
Slice or grate the cheese.

Cheese and Pickle
As above, and mix with a little pickle or chutney.

Cheese Slices
Quick and easy. Use straight from the packet. Spread pickle on top of the cheese if liked.

Cheese and Tomato
Slice a tomato layer on top of the cheese.

Cheese and Onion
Peel and thinly slice an onion, lay it thinly on top of the sliced cheese.

Cold Meat
Sliced, cooked meat, from the supermarket or delicatessen: ham, tongue, turkey roll, chicken roll, salami, garlic sausage, etc. Buy according to your taste and pocket. Buy fresh as you need it; do not store too long in the fridge.

Cold Meat from the Joint
Beef and mustard or horseradish sauce
Slice the beef thinly, and spread with the mustard or horseradish.

Cold Lamb and Mint Sauce
Slice the meat, cut off any excess fat. Add the mint sauce.

Cold Pork and Apple Sauce and Stuffing
Slice the pork, spread with any leftover apple sauce and stuffing.

Cold Chicken
Use up the fiddly bits from a roast chicken or buy chicken roll slices. Spread with cranberry jelly and stuffing. Do not store for too long in the fridge; buy just a little at a time.

Egg
Cook for 10 minutes in boiling water. Shell, wash and mash with a fork. Mix it either with a little mayonnaise or tomato chutney. One egg will fill two rounds of cut bread sandwiches.

Marmite
Very good for you, especially with a chunk of cheese, or topped with sliced cheese.

Peanut Butter
No need to butter the bread first. Top with seedless jam (jelly) if liked.

Salad
Washed lettuce, sliced tomato, sliced cucumber, layered together.

Salmon
Open a can, drain off any excess juice, and tip the salmon into a bowl. Discard the bones and skin, and mash with a little vinegar and pepper. Spread on the buttered bread, top with cucumber slices or lettuce if liked.

Tuna Fish
Open a can, drain off the oil. Tip the tuna fish into a bowl

and mash with vinegar and pepper, or mayonnaise. Spread on the buttered bread, top with lettuce or cucumber slices.

Liver Pâté
Choose from the numerous smooth or rough pâtés in the supermarket. Brown or granary bread is particularly good with pâté.

Eat with your Packed Lunch:
Cottage Cheese (plain or flavoured)
Eat from the carton with a fresh buttered roll, or an apple if you're slimming. Don't forget to take a spoon.

Yoghurt
Eat from the carton – remember to take a spoon.

Hard-boiled Egg
Hard boil an egg. Shell and wash it. Pop it into a polythene bag and eat with a fresh buttered roll.

Scotch Egg
Buy fresh from the supermarket.

FRIED BREAD   *Serves 1*
Best cooked in the frying pan in the fat left from frying bacon or sausages.

Preparation and cooking time: 4–5 minutes.

1–2 slices of bread
Fat left in the pan from cooking sausages or bacon (or 2 tsp cooking oil and large knob of butter)

Remove the sausage or bacon from the pan and keep hot. Cut the bread slices in half, and fry in the hot fat over a moderate heat for 1 to 2 minutes on each side, until golden brown and crispy, adding a little extra butter to the pan if necessary.

FRIED CHEESE SANDWICHES

Serves 1

A very quick and tasty snack.

Preparation and cooking time: 10 minutes.

2–4 slices of bread
½ oz (12g) butter
2–4 thin cheese slices (you can use pre-packed cheese slices if you wish)
1 tbsp cooking oil and a large knob of butter (for frying)

Extra fillings (optional):
1 thinly-sliced tomato
1 tsp pickle
1–2 rashers of crisply fried bacon – fry this ready before you start the sandwiches

Lightly butter the slices of bread. Make them into sandwiches with 1 to 2 slices of cheese in each sandwich, adding any of the optional extras you like.

Heat the oil and knob of butter in a frying pan, over a moderate heat. Put the sandwiches into the hot fat, and fry for a few minutes on each side, until the bread is golden and crispy, and the cheese is beginning to melt.

Remove from the pan, drain on a piece of kitchen paper if they seem a bit greasy. Eat at once while hot.

GARLIC BREAD   *Serves 1*

A sophisticated alternative to hot bread rolls.

Preparation and cooking time: 18–20 minutes.

1 clove of garlic (or ½ tsp garlic powder or paste)
2 oz (50g) butter
½ French loaf or 1–2 bread rolls (according to appetite)
Large piece of cooking foil (for wrapping)

Peel, chop and crush the garlic clove, if used, until smooth.
(You can crush it with a pestle and mortar or garlic press, if
you have one, or use the flat side of a knife but this is more
fiddly.) Cream together the butter and crushed garlic (or
garlic powder or paste), until soft and well-mixed.

Cut the loaf nearly through into 1 in (2.5cm) slices (be
careful not to cut the slices completely or the loaf will drop
into bits) or cut the rolls in half. Butter the slices of the loaf,
or the rolls, generously on both sides with the garlic butter
and press the loaf or rolls together again. Wrap the loaf or
rolls loosely in the foil. Heat the bread in a hot oven (400°F/
200°C/Gas Mark 6–7) until hot and crisp (approximately 5
minutes). Serve at once, with the foil unfolded.

HERB BREAD   *Serves 1*

If you don't like garlic, omit garlic from the above recipe and
make a herb loaf, adding a really generous handful of freshly
chopped or snipped mixed herbs and a tsp lemon juice to the
butter.

CHEESE BREAD

Serves 1

A delicious variation of herb bread, using up odds and ends
of cheese as well.

2 oz (50g) butter
3–4 oz (75–100g) Cheddar, Edam, Double Gloucester, etc.
Handful of fresh herbs – parsley, chives, etc.
1–2 spring onions or ½ tsp very finely chopped onion
    (optional)
½ French loaf or 1–2 rolls (according to appetite)
Large piece of cooking foil (for wrapping)

Beat the butter until soft. Finely grate the cheese and beat it
into the butter, adding washed snipped or chopped herbs and
onions, if used. Slice the bread and fill and bake it as for
Garlic Bread.

CREAM CHEESE LOAF

Serves 1

Use the recipe and method for Cheese Bread, but use 3–4 oz
(75–100g) cream cheese instead of the finely grated hard
cheese. One stick of washed, very finely chopped celery can
be used instead of the onion if you prefer it.

BEANS (OR SPAGHETTI) ON TOAST   *Serves 1*

Just in case you've never cooked these before, here is the method.

Preparation and cooking time: 5 minutes.

1 oz (25g) cheese (optional)
1 small (8 oz/225g) tin beans, spaghetti, spaghetti hoops, etc.
2–3 slices of bread
Butter

Grate the cheese, or chop it finely (if used).

Put the beans or spaghetti into a small saucepan, and heat slowly over a moderate heat, stirring occasionally. Toast the bread and spread one side of it with butter. When the beans are beginning to bubble, stir gently until they are thoroughly heated.

Put the toast onto a warm plate, and pour the beans on top of the buttered side (some people prefer the toast left at the side of the plate). Sprinkle the cheese on top. Eat at once.

GARLIC MUSHROOMS

Serves 1

Delicious, but don't breathe over other people after eating these! Serve with fried bacon to make a more substantial meal.

Preparation and cooking time: 10 minutes.

3–4 oz (75–100g) mushrooms
1 clove of fresh garlic (or garlic powder or garlic paste)
1–2 rashers of bacon (optional)
1 oz (25g) butter with 1 tsp cooking oil
2 thick slices of bread

Wash the mushrooms. Peel, chop and crush the fresh garlic, if used. Fry the bacon and keep hot. Melt the butter and oil in a saucepan over a moderate heat. Add the garlic (fresh, powder or paste) and mushrooms.

Stir well, and fry gently for 3 to 5 minutes, stirring and spooning the garlic-flavoured butter over the mushrooms. While the mushrooms are cooking, toast the bread lightly, cut in half and put onto a hot plate. Spoon the mushrooms onto the toast and pour the remaining garlic butter over the top. Top with bacon, if used. Eat at once.

MUSHROOMS A LA GREQUE

Serves 2 or 1 hungry person

This can be a vegetable accompaniment or a delicious snack or light lunch.

Preparation and cooking time: 30 minutes.

4 oz (100g) mushrooms
1 small onion
1 clove of garlic or ¼ tsp minced garlic
1 tbsp olive oil or vegetable oil
½ vegetable stock cube
½ cup boiling water
¼ tsp vegetable extract
1 tbsp white wine or cider
2 tsp tomato purée or ketchup
½ tsp mixed herbs
Salt and pepper
Few sprigs of fresh parsley or chives
Paprika or cayenne pepper (for garnish)

Heat the oven to 325°F/170°C/Gas Mark 3–4.

Wash and thickly slice the mushrooms (leave tiny button mushrooms whole) and put into a casserole dish. Peel and slice the onion and garlic. Heat the oil in a saucepan over a gentle heat and fry the onion and garlic for 4 to 5 minutes until softened. Spoon this over the mushrooms.

Dissolve the stock cube in the boiling water, add the vegetable extract, wine or cider, tomato purée or ketchup, and pour over the vegetables.

Sprinkle with mixed herbs, season to taste with salt and pepper. Wash and scissor-snip parsley or chives over the dish. Bake in the hot oven for 15 to 20 minutes until the mushrooms are soft. Sprinkle with paprika or cayenne, depending on whether you like it hot, and serve.

PIZZA

There are so many makes, shapes and sizes of pizza available now, both fresh and frozen, that it hardly seems worth the effort of making your own. However, these commercial ones are usually improved by adding your own extras during the cooking, either when under the grill or in the oven according to the instructions on the packet.

Add these extras for the last 5 to 10 minutes of cooking time by spreading them on top of the pizza:

Cheese
Use grated or thinly sliced.

Ham
Chop and sprinkle over the pizza.

Salami, Garlic Sausage
Chop or fold slices and arrange on top of the pizza.

Mushrooms
Wash and slice thinly, spread over the pizza.

Tomatoes
Slice thinly, spread over the pizza.

Olives
A few spread on top add colour and flavour.

Anchovies or Sardines
Arrange criss-cross over the pizza.

QUICK SAVOURY PANCAKES *Makes 6–8 pancakes*

Use up any leftover Bolognese or chilli sauce for a quick supper dish.

Preparation and cooking time: 30 minutes.

Pancake batter:
4 oz (100g) plain flour
Pinch of salt
1 egg
2 cups (½ pt/300ml) milk
2–3 tbsp oil (for frying)

Filling:
2 cups (½ pt/300ml) cooked Bolognese or chilli sauce
2 cups (½ pt/300ml) homemade or bought tomato sauce (use the sauces you can buy for casseroles)
Parsley or watercress (for garnish)

Make the pancakes: Mix the flour and salt in a bowl, beat in the egg and gradually beat in the milk to make a thin batter. Heat a little oil in an omelette or frying pan, and, when hot, pour in enough batter just to cover the base thinly. Cook for 1 to 2 minutes until firm, then toss or turn and cook the other side. Slide onto a plate and keep warm in a low oven (200°F/100°C/Gas Mark 1), and fry the remaining pancakes.

Put the chosen Bolognese or chilli sauce into a saucepan and heat gently until piping hot, cooking right through not just warming up.

Put the hot pancakes onto a clean worktop and divide the hot filling between them. Roll up the pancakes and place them on a hot serving dish in the warm oven. Heat the chosen tomato sauce in the saucepan and when really hot pour over the pancakes. Garnish with parsley or watercress and serve.

CRUDITÉS
Serves 1

Nice as a starter or light snack. Use a good variety of raw vegetables cut into finger-sized sticks or bite-sized chunks, and serve the dip in little individual pots or dishes.

Preparation and cooking time: 10–15 minutes.

For each serving prepare a small stack of several different raw vegetables, and one or two pots of dips.

Vegetables:
1 carrot
One 2 in (5cm) length of cucumber
1–2 sticks of celery
½ small red or green pepper, cut lengthways
Few cauliflower florets
Few radishes
3 or 4 mushrooms
Few tiny spring onions

Dips:
2–3 tbsp mayonnaise, either plain or flavoured as below
Crisp lettuce or watercress (for garnish)

Prepare the vegetables: Peel the carrot and cut into sticks. Wash the cucumber and cut lengthways into sticks. Trim and wash the celery and cut into thin lengths. Wash the pepper and remove the seeds, cut in half lengthways and slice into fingers. Wash the cauliflower, break carefully into small florets. Wash and slice the mushrooms if large. Trim and wash the spring onions.

Mix the chosen mayonnaise with different chosen flavourings:

Garlic: Beat in ¼ tsp garlic paste or powder
Curry: Beat in ¼ tsp curry powder, cayenne pepper or few drops hot pepper sauce
Rosé: Beat in ½ tsp tomato purée or ketchup

63

Blue cheese: Beat 1 oz (25g) blue cheese to a paste, and mix it into the mayonnaise.

Spoon the dips into individual pots. Serve the crudités on a plate, with the pot of dip surrounded by little piles of vegetables, garnished with washed crisp lettuce or watercress. For a party, serve large dishes of dips, with crudités, crisps or pieces of pitta bread.

BASIC GREEN SALAD

Serves 1

Preparation time: 5 minutes.

3–4 washed lettuce leaves
½ small onion
1 tbsp vinaigrette

Leave the lettuce leaves whole if small, or shred as finely as you like. Peel and slice the onion. Put the lettuce and onion into a salad bowl, add the vinaigrette and lightly turn the lettuce over in the dressing, until well mixed.

Other salad vegetables can be added:

Beetroot (cooked, if necessary, and sliced)
Celery (washed, scraped, if necessary, cut into 1 in (2.5cm) lengths)
Cucumber (washed, cut into rings or chunks)
Pepper (washed, cored, cut into rings)
Radishes (with tops cut off, roots removed and washed)
Spring onion (washed, cut off roots and yellow leaves, cut into rings or leave whole)
Tomatoes (washed, sliced or cut into quarters)
Watercress, mustard and cress (washed, sprinkled on top of the other vegetables).

WARM LETTUCE AND PEANUT SALAD *Serves 1–2*

This is different from the usual salad mixture. I like to use the 'fancy' lettuces for this: endive, radiccio, webb, cos or even Chinese leaves. Supermarkets sell prepared mixtures of these lettuces, which is an economical way of buying several different types of lettuce in small amounts, and these are excellent for this recipe.

Preparation and cooking time: 10 minutes.

Portion of lettuce – a mixture of colours and textures looks most attractive
1 thick slice of wholemeal or white bread
2 tbsp oil – both olive and walnut oil have a lovely flavour, but any vegetable oil is acceptable
2 tsp wine vinegar
2 tbsp (2 oz/50g) salted peanuts

Wash and thoroughly dry the lettuce, shred it coarsely and put it into a salad bowl. Cut the bread into ½ in (1cm) cubes. Heat the oil in a frying pan over a moderate heat and fry the bread cubes for a few minutes, turning frequently, until evenly browned and crispy.

Dress the lettuce by tossing it in the wine vinegar, then pour over the fried bread cubes and any oil left in the pan. Add the peanuts and turn the mixture well in the bowl. Serve at once, while still warm.

Note: 1–2 rashers of crisply fried bacon can be chopped and sprinkled over the salad. Fry the bacon before the bread, and add with the peanuts.

RICE SALAD

Serves 2 or more

The cold version of fried rice. It can be made into a light meal with lots of extras, or left plainer as an accompaniment.

Preparation and cooking time: 15 minutes.

2 cups cooked rice (you will need to cook 1 cup/4 oz/100g dry rice if there's none ready cooked – see page 118)
4 tbsp French dressing (bought or mix 3 tbsp oil with 1 tbsp wine vinegar or lemon juice, pinch of sugar, salt, pepper)
½ small onion or 3–4 spring onions
2 oz (50g) frozen mixed vegetables and/or peas, cooked and drained
2 oz (50g) canned sweetcorn, drained
Few sprigs fresh parsley and/or chives

Extras:
2 oz (50g) mushrooms, washed and sliced
Few rings of green or red peppers, chopped
1 hard-boiled egg, cut into chunks
Small piece of cucumber, diced
1 or 2 tomatoes, roughly chopped or chunked
2 tbsp canned kidney, flageolet or aduki beans, well drained
Handful black or green olives
2 oz (50g) cooked, peeled prawns
2 oz (50g) cooked ham, chicken, etc., diced

Put the cooked rice into a serving bowl. Stir the French dressing well, then pour it over the rice and mix all together. Peel and finely chop the onion, or trim and chop the spring onions, and stir into the rice with the cooked mixed vegetables and sweetcorn. Add the chosen extras and mix gently. Cover with cling film and leave in a cool place until ready to serve; this salad will benefit from standing for at least 30 minutes to absorb all the different flavours. To serve, stir the salad again and top with a little fresh snipped parsley or chives.

PASTA SALAD

Serves 1, 2 or more

Serve as a salad accompaniment, or add cold cooked meat, sausage, salami, tuna fish or prawns to make it into a complete light meal. You can use up any cooked pasta shapes (shells, bows, etc.) that you have left over.

Preparation time: 15 minutes.

Per person:

1 cup (4 oz/100g) cooked pasta (if you need to cook the pasta allow 2 oz (50g) dry pasta per person)

For each cup of cooked pasta allow a mixture of the following:
1 tbsp finely chopped onion
1 tomato, cut in chunks
1–2 rings of green or red pepper, chopped
2 tbsp tomato- or curry-flavoured mayonnaise
1–2 oz (25–50g) cooked chicken, turkey, ham, salami or sausage
1–2 tbsp drained, canned tuna fish or cooked prawns
Few green or black olives (stoned)
Parsley (for garnish)

Put the cooked pasta into a bowl, mix in the chopped onion, tomato and peppers, add the flavoured mayonnaise and turn the mixture over gently until everything is well coated.

Slice the meat (if used) into bite-sized pieces or dice, and mix in to the salad, or mix in the tuna or prawns if used.

Turn the salad into a serving dish, garnish with the olives and snipped parsley, then cover and leave to chill for at least 30 minutes if possible to absorb the flavours before serving.

GREEK SALAD

Usually served as a side dish, but the cheese makes it filling enough to have a nice large helping as a light lunch on a hot day.

Preparation time: 10 minutes.

½ small onion
1 tbsp vinaigrette dressing
2 in (5cm) chunk of cucumber
1–2 tomatoes
Few black olives
2 oz (50g) Greek Feta cheese – if you can't get Feta, use a
   crumbly white cheese; Lancashire is good

Peel and slice the onion, and put into a basin with the vinaigrette dressing. Peel the cucumber, cut into dice. Wash and slice the tomatoes. Add the cucumber and tomatoes to the onion mixture with the olives, stirring well to mix with the dressing. Dice the cheese. Pour the salad into a serving dish, sprinkle the cheese dice over the top.

Serve as a side salad or with warm pitta bread or bread rolls as a light lunch.

CREOLE SALAD

This salad is a good way to use up leftovers, cooked rice, etc. If you want to make a smaller amount, just use less rice and cut down on the amount of fruit, nuts and dressing.

Try to make it at least one hour before eating so that the salad can absorb the flavour from the mayonnaise.

Preparation and cooking time: 30 minutes (or 15 minutes if rice is already cooked).

1 cup uncooked brown or patna (long grain type) rice or 2 cups cooked rice
1–2 bananas
1 red or green eating apple (leave the skin on)
1–2 tbsp lemon juice (juice of ½ lemon; use the rest in the dressing)
Tiny bunch of seedless grapes
1–2 slices of pineapple
2 tbsp sultanas
½ cup chopped walnuts or pecan nuts
1 tbsp grated coconut (optional)

Dressing:
3–4 tbsp mayonnaise
1 tbsp lemon juice (use the rest of the lemon)
Shake of tabasco sauce
½ tsp mustard

Cook the rice (see page 118), drain, rinse and leave to cool.
Peel and slice the bananas. Wash, core and slice the apple (do not peel). Turn these slices of fruit in the lemon juice to stop them going brown. Wash the grapes. Cut the pineapple into small pieces. Wash the sultanas and drain. Mix the fruit and nuts with the cooked rice.

The Dressing
Mix the mayonnaise with all the other dressing ingredients, seasoning to taste with the tabasco sauce. Stir the

mayonnaise mixture thoroughly into the rice mixture. Tip into a serving dish, sprinkle with coconut if liked. Cover the dish and leave in the fridge until needed.

This salad looks attractive served on a flat dish or on a bed of washed lettuce or watercress, but it is supposed to be a white salad, so do not sprinkle with parsley.

POTATO SALAD

You can use up any leftover boiled potatoes you may have lurking in the fridge in this recipe, or you could cook some potatoes specially for it.

You will need 1–2 potatoes per person (more if they're tiny new ones).

Slice the boiled old or new potatoes into large bite-sized chunks. Mix the potato pieces with mayonnaise (you will need approximately 1 tbsp mayonnaise for each person), turning the potatoes over until all the pieces are coated.

Cut 1 or 2 shelled hard-boiled eggs into chunks and mix them in gently, adding a handful of washed, snipped parsley, chives or spring onions. Pile the salad into a serving dish and garnish with a little more snipped fresh herbs.

SAVOURY FRUIT SALAD
Serves 2–4

An intriguing taste of sweet and savoury, which can also be an accompaniment to other hot or cold dishes.

Preparation and cooking time: 15 minutes.

½ small onion or 2–3 spring onions
2 sticks of celery
Small bunch of seedless grapes
2 oz (50g/2 tbsp) walnut halves
1 green eating apple
1 red eating apple
1 eating pear
1 tbsp lemon juice
1–2 tbsp vinaigrette dressing

Peel the onion and cut it into thin rings, or wash, trim and slice the spring onions. Wash and trim the celery, and cut into ½ in (1cm) lengths. Wash the grapes and drain well. Roughly chop the walnuts. Wash the apples, cut into quarters and remove the cores, slice thinly and place in a bowl. Peel, core and thinly slice the pear, and mix with the apple. Stir in the lemon juice and mix thoroughly to coat the fruit to stop it browning.

Add the onion, celery, grapes and walnuts to the fruit. Pour over the vinaigrette dressing and toss lightly. Cover with cling film and chill in the fridge until needed.

MIXED BEAN SALAD

Make at least enough for two people, so that you can use a good mixture of ingredients. This is a good recipe for using up the odds and ends of leftover canned beans.

Preparation time: 10 minutes.

2 tbsp canned kidney beans
2 tbsp canned white beans (Barlotti, Cannellini or haricot)
1 tbsp canned chick peas
2 tbsp canned sweetcorn (the canned sweetcorn with pepper is rather nice)
½ small onion or 1–2 spring onions
1 stick of celery
1 tbsp vinaigrette dressing
Salt and pepper
Few sprigs of parsley or chives

Rinse the canned beans and chick peas in cold water, drain them and put them with the peas and sweetcorn into a basin.

Peel and finely chop the onion or trim, wash and slice the spring onion. Wash and chop the celery, and add the onion and celery to the bean mixture.

Stir in the vinaigrette dressing, mix well and spoon into a serving dish or individual side dishes. Sprinkle with washed, snipped parsley and chives.

TABBOULEH

Serves 1–2 according to appetite

This salad makes a more unusual accompaniment at buffet meals or barbecues. Tabbouleh will keep for a few days in a covered bowl in the fridge.

Preparation time: 10 minutes (plus 1 hour for soaking).

4 oz (100g/4 very heaped tbsp) bulgar or cracked wheat
3–4 spring onions
Small bunch of chives ⎫
Small bunch of parsley ⎬ **Use a mixture of herbs; it**
Small bunch of mint ⎭ **should be as green as possible**
2–3 tbsp olive oil or vegetable oil
2 tbsp lemon juice (juice of ½ lemon)
Salt and pepper

Put the bulgar or cracked wheat in a bowl, half fill the bowl with cold water and leave the wheat to soak for an hour.

Strain well in a sieve, and squeeze as dry as possible. Dry the bowl and tip the wheat back into it.

Trim and wash the spring onions (cut off the roots and any yellow leaves, leaving as much of the green as looks appetising). Chop or scissor-snip the onions into the wheat. Wash and scissor-snip the chives and parsley into the wheat. Strip the leaves off the mint stalks, rinse the leaves in cold water and chop or scissor-snip them finely into the wheat mixture. Mix the wheat and herbs well together, add the oil and season to taste with the lemon juice, salt and pepper.

AVOCADO SALAD
Fills one avocado half

This must be my daughter's favourite lunch; she has it so often. It also makes a good starter, if you're entertaining friends, using small avocados. You can use any variety of salad vegetables available, but it's quite economical as you only need a very little of each to make a good filling. It looks nice served in a glass avocado dish or a small wooden bowl, garnished with lettuce or Chinese leaves.

Preparation time: 10 minutes.

Use a mixture of your favourite salad ingredients:
1 tomato
Small piece of green pepper
Small piece of red pepper
Small stalk of celery
2–3 rings of onion
1–2 spring onions
Small piece of carrot
Handful of fresh chives
½ large avocado pear
1 oz (25g) Cheddar, Edam, Double Gloucester, etc. cheese
1–2 tsp lemon juice or vinaigrette dressing

Prepare the salad vegetables according to their type: Wash and chop the tomato, peppers and celery. Peel and very finely chop the onion. Trim and slice the spring onion. Peel and coarsely grate or finely chop the carrot. Wash and scissor-snip the chives, and mix all the vegetables together in a basin.

Halve the avocado, remove the stone and scoop out some of the avocado flesh with a teaspoon, but leave enough flesh on the skin to ensure a firm shell. Chop the scooped-out avocado into cubes. (If you are making this in advance, toss the cubed avocado in lemon juice and brush the avocado shell with lemon juice to stop them browning.) Add the avocado to the vegetables.

Coarsely grate or cube the chosen cheese and add to the

vegetable mixture. Mix in the lemon juice or vinaigrette dressing, and spoon the filling into the avocado shell. Serve immediately or cover the filled avocado with cling film and leave in the fridge until needed.

WINTER SALAD
Serves 1

Trim, shred and wash a quarter of a white or green cabbage. Drain well and dry in a salad shaker (if you have one) or put into a clean tea-towel and shake or pat dry. Put the cabbage in a dish, with any other salad vegetables, such as raw, grated carrot, tomato quarters, cucumber, celery, peppers, peeled sliced onion.

It can either be served on its own, or with a dressing made from the following ingredients mixed together thoroughly: 4 tsp salad oil, 2 tsp vinegar, pinch of salt, pepper and sugar.

COLESLAW
Serves 1

A quick and tasty way of using up extra raw cabbage. Serve with cold meat, or with hot dishes.

Preparation time: 15 minutes.

¼ crisp white cabbage
1 small carrot
1 eating apple (red-skinned if possible)
Lemon juice (if possible)
1 small onion
1–2 tbsp mayonnaise
Salt and pepper

Trim off the outer leaves and stalk of the cabbage. Shred it finely, wash it well in cold water. Scrape the carrot. Chop it finely or grate it. Peel and core the apple. Chop it finely or grate it. Sprinkle with a little lemon juice. Peel the onion. Chop or grate it finely. Drain the cabbage well.

Mix all the vegetables together in a bowl. Toss lightly in the mayonnaise until all the ingredients are well-coated. Season to taste.

Many different fruit or vegetables can be used in this recipe. A few chopped salted nuts, a tbsp of washed, dried sultanas, a little chopped green pepper are some ideas you might like to try.

5
Vegetables, Vegetable Dishes and Rice

This chapter gives basic instructions on preparing and cooking fresh vegetables (listed in alphabetical order) to be eaten as part of a meal, together with recipes using vegetables which are substantial enough to be used as a lunch or supper dish by themselves.

When cooking vegetables in water, remember that a lot of the goodness and flavour soaks from the vegetables into the cooking water. So do not use too much water or overcook them. When possible, use the vegetable water for making gravy. Frozen vegetables are convenient but are generally dearer than fresh vegetables. Vegetable prices vary tremendously according to the season, so look out for the best buys at the vegetable counter.

GLOBE ARTICHOKES

2. Globe Artichokes

These are the green, leafy type of artichoke. They look large, but as you only eat the bottom tip of each leaf, you do need *a whole artichoke for each person*. As they are expensive, cook them mainly for special·occasions.

Cut off the stem of the artichoke to make the base level, snip off the points of the leaves, and wash the artichoke well in cold water. Put in a large saucepan, cover with boiling salted water, and boil for 30 to 40 minutes, until a leaf will pull off easily.

Drain the water from the pan and then turn the artichoke upside down in the pan for a few moments to drain any remaining water. Serve with plenty of butter.

JERUSALEM ARTICHOKES

3. Jerusalem Artichokes

These artichokes look like knobbly potatoes. Cook them immediately they are peeled, as they go brown very quickly even in cold water. A little lemon juice in the cooking water helps to keep them white.

8 oz (225g) serves 1–2 portions.

BOILED

Peel the artichokes and cut them into evenly-sized lumps about the size of small potatoes. Boil them in a pan of salted water for 20 to 30 minutes, until tender. Drain and serve with a dab of butter.

BOILED WITH CHICKEN SAUCE

Cook in salted water (as above) until tender. Drain, and put back in the saucepan with ½ can (10 oz/300g size) of condensed chicken soup. Bring back to the boil, stirring occasionally. Tip the artichokes onto a warm plate, pouring the chicken sauce over them.

FRIED

Peel the artichokes and cut them into thick slices or chunks. Put 1 tsp cooking oil and ½ oz (12g) butter into a frying pan, add the artichoke pieces and cook gently, turning frequently, for 15 to 20 minutes, until soft. Tip the artichokes onto a warm plate, pouring the buttery sauce over them.

ASPARAGUS

A very expensive treat! *Usually sold in bundles, enough for 2–4 servings.*

Cut off the woody ends of the stems and then scrape off the white tough parts of the stems. Rinse. Tie the stems into a bundle, with clean string or white cotton, and stand them tips uppermost in a pan with 1 in (2.5cm) boiling water. Cover the pan with a lid or a dome of foil, and boil for 8 to 10 minutes, until tender. Remove them carefully from the pan. Asparagus is traditionally eaten with the fingers. To eat, just dip the tips in butter and leave any woody parts that still remain on the stems.

AUBERGINES

The English name for the aubergine is the 'egg plant'. These lovely, shiny purple-skinned vegetables are best left unpeeled.

Fry 1 medium-sized aubergine per person.

To get rid of any bitter taste before cooking, slice the aubergine into ½ in (1.25cm) pieces. Put into a colander or strainer (if you do not have one, lay the slices on a piece of kitchen paper), sprinkle with salt, press a heavy plate down on top and leave for 30 minutes so that the bitter juices are pressed out. Wash and dry the slices. Heat a little oil in a frying pan, and fry gently until soft (about 5 minutes).

GREEK-STYLE STUFFED AUBERGINES   *Serves 2*

Allow a whole aubergine per person for a main meal, served with vegetables or salad, or serve half an aubergine each for a substantial and unusual starter. You can use cooked mince beef in this recipe, as long as you don't serve it to a traditional Greek cook!

Preparation and cooking time: 35 minutes
plus 30 minutes draining time.

For each aubergine allow:
1 oz (25g) butter and 1 tsp olive oil
½ small onion
1 clove of garlic
1 tomato (squashy ones are fine)
2 oz (50g) cooked lamb
1 tsp lemon juice
Salt, black pepper, cayenne pepper (optional)
¼ tsp mixed herbs, pinch oregano and/or basil, sprig of parsley
1 tsp grated Parmesan cheese

Wash the aubergines, cut them in half lengthways. Loosen the flesh from the sides of the skin and cut across the flesh several times. Sprinkle with salt and place cut-side-down in a colander on a plate. Leave to drain for 20 to 30 minutes to get rid of the bitter juices.

Heat the oven to 400°F/200°C/Gas Mark 6–7. Rinse and dry the aubergines, arrange them cut-side-up in a greased ovenproof dish, dot with half the butter, cover with a lid or cooking foil and bake for 15 to 20 minutes until soft.

Meanwhile, peel and finely chop the onion and garlic, and wash and chop the tomato. Mince or finely chop the lamb. Heat the remaining butter with the olive oil in a pan over a moderate heat and fry the onion and garlic for 3 to 4 minutes until soft. Add the chopped tomato and cook for a further 2 to 3 minutes. Stir in the minced lamb, season to taste with the lemon juice, salt, pepper, and herbs, and heat gently until the mixture is hot.

Take the aubergines from the oven and allow to cool slightly. Then carefully scoop the cooked aubergine from the centres, leaving enough flesh to make a firm case. Dice the aubergine and stir it into the hot meat mixture. Adjust the seasoning. Pile the hot stuffing into the aubergine cases, sprinkle with the grated Parmesan cheese and reheat in the hot oven for 5 to 10 minutes until golden and bubbling.

AVOCADO PEARS

Buy avocados when the price is down – the price varies considerably during the year, as they are imported from several countries. They make a nourishing change.

Choose pears that yield slightly when pressed gently. Unripe pears feel very hard.

Slice the avocado in half lengthways, cutting through to the stone. Then separate the two halves by twisting gently. Remove the stone with the tip of the knife, trying not to damage the flesh, which should be soft and buttery in texture.

Cut avocados discolour very quickly, so prepare them just before serving, or rub the cut halves with lemon juice to stop them going brown. Serve avocados plain with a squeeze of lemon juice, with a vinaigrette dressing or with any one of the numerous fillings spooned into the cavity from where the stone was removed. Brown bread and butter is the traditional accompaniment, with a garnish of lettuce, tomato and cucumber.

Some Filling Ideas
Vinaigrette
Mix well 2 tsp oil, 1 tsp vinegar, salt, pepper and a pinch of sugar.

Mayonnaise
1 tbsp mayonnaise.

Cottage Cheese
Mix well together 2 tbsp cottage cheese (plain or with chives, pineapple, etc.) and 1 tsp mayonnaise.

Prawn or Shrimp
Mix gently together 1–2 tbsp shelled prawns or shrimps (fresh, frozen or canned), 1 tbsp mayonnaise and/or cottage cheese. A sauce can also be made with a mixture of 1 tbsp salad cream and a dash of tomato ketchup.

Egg
Shell and chop 1 hard-boiled egg. Mix gently with 1 tbsp mayonnaise and/or cottage cheese.

Yoghurt
2 tbsp yoghurt on its own, or mixed with a chopped tomato and a few slices chopped cucumber.

CREAMY AVOCADO TOAST   *Serves 1*
Use a soft avocado pear for this. They are often sold off cheaply when they become very ripe and the shop wants to sell them quickly.

Preparation time: 5 minutes.

1 ripe avocado
Salt and pepper
2 thick slices of bread (brown or granary)
Knob of butter

Cut the avocado in half, lengthways and remove the stone. Scoop out the soft flesh with a teaspoon, put it into a small basin, and mash to a soft cream. Season with the salt and pepper.

Toast the bread on both sides, spread one side with butter, then spread the avocado cream thickly on the top. Eat while the toast is hot.

SAVOURY AVOCADO SNACK

Serves 1

If you're a vegetarian and don't want to eat bacon, you may prefer to sprinkle ½ tbsp chopped walnuts on top of the cheese instead.

Preparation and cooking time: 15 minutes.

1–2 rashers of bacon
Oil (for frying)
1 small avocado pear
1 oz (25g) cheese
Chunk of French bread
Knob of butter

De-rind the bacon. Fry it in a little oil in a frying pan over a moderate heat until crisp.

Peel the avocado pear and slice it, removing the stone. Grate or slice the cheese.

Cut the French bread in half lengthways, and spread with the butter. Arrange layers of the avocado and bacon on the bread. Top with the cheese slices or grated cheese.

Grill under a hot grill for a few minutes, until the cheese is golden, bubbling and melted. Eat at once.

BAKED AVOCADO

Serves 1

Sprinkle the spare half of the avocado with lemon juice to stop it browning, wrap it in cling film and store it in the fridge for tomorrow's lunch. Leave the stone in; the pear will keep better.

Preparation and cooking time: 20–25 minutes.

½ large, ripe avocado pear
1 tsp lemon juice
1 oz (25g) Cheddar or Edam cheese
Few sprigs of fresh chives or 1–2 spring onions
Few sprigs of fresh parsley
1 heaped tbsp pine kernels or chopped walnuts, pecan nuts or hazelnuts
2 tsp canned or cooked sweetcorn
1 tbsp white wine or cider
Salt and pepper
Cayenne or paprika pepper

Heat the oven to 400°F/200°C/Gas Mark 6–7. Place the half avocado on a lightly greased oven-proof dish and sprinkle the cut surface with lemon juice to stop browning. (Store the spare half as above.)

Grate the cheese into a small basin, wash the chives and scissor-snip them into the grated cheese, or wash and trim the spring onion (trim off the roots and yellow leaves, but retain as much of the green as looks appetising) and chop or snip the onion into the cheese.

Wash and scissor-snip the parsley into the cheese mixture. Add the pine kernels or chopped nuts and sweetcorn, and mix together with wine or cider. Season with salt, pepper and a little lemon juice to taste.

Pile the mixture into the avocado (it will heap up on top of the pear). Bake in the hot oven for 10 to 15 minutes until golden brown and bubbling. Serve with crispy bread rolls or hot garlic bread.

BROAD BEANS

Buy 4–8 oz (100–225g) unshelled beans per person, according to the size of the beans. The smaller, younger beans go further, as you can cook them whole, like French beans, whereas older, larger beans need to be shelled.

TINY NEW BROAD BEANS

Top and tail the beans with a vegetable knife or a pair of scissors. Either leave them whole or cut them into shorter lengths (4 in/10cm) depending on their size. Boil them in water for 5 to 10 minutes, according to size, until tender. Drain and serve with a knob of butter.

LARGER BROAD BEANS

Remove the beans from the pods. Cook in boiling water for 5 to 10 minutes, until tender. Drain and serve with a knob of butter, or parsley sauce, if you feel very ambitious.

FROZEN BROAD BEANS

Allow approximately 4 oz (100g) per serving. Cook as instructed on the packet, and serve as above.

FRENCH BEANS

Can be rather expensive, but as there is very little waste you need only buy a small amount. *Allow approximately 4 oz (100g) per serving.*

Top and tail the beans with a vegetable knife or a pair of scissors. Wash the beans and cut the longer beans in half (about 4 in/10cm). Put them into a pan of boiling, salted water and cook for 2 to 5 minutes, until just tender. Drain well and serve them with a knob of butter.

FROZEN WHOLE FRENCH BEANS

Allow approximately 3–4 oz (75–100g) per serving. Cook in boiling, salted water as directed on the packet and serve as above with a knob of butter. Very tasty, but be careful not to overcook them.

RUNNER BEANS

These are sold frozen and ready to cook all year round, but lovely fresh beans are available in August and September. Choose crisp, green beans; limp, pallid ones are not as fresh as they should be. *Allow 4 oz (100g) beans per person.*

Top and tail the beans. Cut down the sides of the large beans to remove any tough stringy bits, and slice the beans evenly into whatever size you prefer, up to 1 in (2.5cm) long. Wash them in cold water. Cook in boiling, salted water for 5 to 10 minutes, according to size, until just tender. Drain well and serve hot.

FROZEN BEANS

Allow 3–4 oz (75–100g) per serving. Cook according to the instructions on the packet, in boiling, salted water.

BEAN SPROUTS

These can be cooked on their own, but are better when cooked with a mixture of stir-fried vegetables. *Allow 4 oz (100g) per portion.* Soak for 10 minutes in cold water, then drain the bean sprouts well. Heat 1 tbsp oil in a frying pan or a wok, add the bean sprouts and fry for 1 to 2 minutes, stirring all the time. Serve at once.

BROCCOLI

Green broccoli and purple sprouting broccoli are both cooked in the same way. *Allow 2–3 pieces or 8 oz (225g) per serving.*

Remove any coarse outer leaves and cut off the ends of the stalks. Wash well in cold water. Boil for 5 to 10 minutes in salted water, until tender. Drain well; press out the water gently with a fork if necessary. Serve with a knob of butter.

FROZEN BROCCOLI

Allow 4–6 oz (100–150g) per serving, according to appetite. Cook as directed on the packet, in boiling, salted water.

BRUSSELS SPROUTS

Try to buy firm, green sprouts of approximately the same size. Yellow outside leaves are a sign of old age.

Allow 4–6 oz (100-150g) per serving.

Cut off the stalk ends, and trim off the outer leaves if necessary. Wash well. Cook in boiling, salted water for 5 to 10 minutes, until tender. Drain well.

FROZEN SPROUTS

Allow 3–4 oz (75–100g) per serving. Cook in boiling, salted water as directed on the packet.

WHITE OR GREEN CABBAGE

A much maligned vegetable, evoking memories of school days. If cooked properly, cabbage is really delicious and much cheaper than a lot of other vegetables. Cabbage goes a very long way, so either buy a *small cabbage* and use it for several meals (cooked, or raw in a winter salad) or *just buy half or a quarter of a cabbage*.

Trim off the outer leaves and the stalk. Cut into quarters and shred, not too finely, removing the central core and cutting that into small pieces. Wash the cabbage. Boil it in salted water for 2 to 5 minutes. Do not overcook. Drain well, serve with a knob of butter, or with a cheese sauce.

To make cabbage cheese, instead of cauliflower cheese, substitute the cabbage for the cauliflower on page 46.

CRISPY CABBAGE CASSEROLE

Serves 1

This is filling enough to serve as a cheap supper dish, with hot bread rolls, butter and a chunk of cheese. It is delicious as a vegetable accompaniment with meat.

Preparation and cooking time: 35 minutes.

1 portion of cabbage (¼ of a cabbage)
1 small onion
1–2 sticks of celery
1 tsp oil and ½ oz (12g) butter (for frying)
1 slice of bread

For the white sauce (or use 1 packet of sauce mix):
2 tsp cornflour (or flour)
1 cup (¼ pt/150ml) milk
½ oz (12g) butter (or margarine)
Salt and pepper

Grease an oven-proof dish or casserole. Trim the outer leaves and stalk from the cabbage. Shred it, not too finely, wash it well and drain. Peel and chop the onion. Scrape and wash the celery and cut into 1 in (2.5cm) lengths. Heat the oil and butter in a frying pan, and fry the onion gently for 2 to 3 minutes until soft. Add the celery and drained cabbage, fry gently for a further 5 minutes, stirring occasionally.

Heat the oven at (400°F/200°C/Gas Mark 6–7). Make the white sauce (see page 231). Put the vegetable mixture into the greased dish. Pour the white sauce over the top. Crumble or grate the bread into crumbs, and sprinkle these on top of the sauce. Dot with a knob of butter. Bake for 15 minutes in the hot oven until the top is crunchy and golden brown.

RED CABBAGE

Usually cooked in a casserole, to make a lovely warming winter vegetable dish. Why not put some jacket potatoes in the oven to eat with it?

Preparation and cooking time: 1 hour (cooked on top of the stove); 1 hour 15 minutes (cooked in the oven).

1 rasher of bacon (optional)
1 small onion
½ small red cabbage
1 eating apple
1 tsp oil
½ oz (12g) butter
Salt and pepper
1 tsp sugar (brown if possible, but white will do)
1 tsp vinegar
½ cup boiling water

Chop the bacon with a sharp knife or a pair of scissors. Peel and chop the onion. Cut off the stalk from the cabbage. Remove any battered outside leaves. Shred the cabbage finely, wash and drain. Peel, core and slice the apple. Melt the oil and butter in a frying pan and fry the bacon until crisp. Remove the bacon, put it on a plate. Add the onion to the pan and fry gently for 2 to 3 minutes, until soft.

PAN METHOD
In a saucepan, put layers of the cabbage, apple, onion and bacon, seasoning each layer with salt, pepper, sugar and vinegar. Pour ½ cup of boiling water over it and lightly sprinkle with sugar. Put on the saucepan lid and simmer gently for 45 minutes, stirring occasionally.

OVEN METHOD
Use a casserole dish (with a lid) that can be put in the oven. Put the vegetables in layers as in the pan method, adding ½ cup of boiling water and the sugar and cook in the oven

(350°F/180°C/Gas Mark 4), stirring occasionally, for about an hour. Jacket potatoes can be cooked with the casserole. Serve hot. Red cabbage cooked in this way is tasty with pork and lamb.

CARROTS

New carrots can simply be scrubbed and cooked whole, like new potatoes. Older, larger carrots should be scraped or peeled, then cut in halves, quarters, slices, rings or dice, as preferred. The smaller the pieces the quicker the carrots will cook.

Allow 4 oz (100g) per serving.

Scrub, peel and slice the carrots as necessary. Boil them in salted water for 5 to 20 minutes, according to their size, until just tender. Serve with a knob of butter.

BUTTERED CARROTS

Prepare the carrots as above: leaving tender, young carrots whole, or slicing old carrots into rings. Put the carrots in a saucepan, with ½ a cup of water, ½ oz (12g) butter, 1 tsp sugar and a pinch of salt. Bring to the boil, then reduce the heat and simmer for 20 minutes, until the carrots are tender. Take the lid off the saucepan, turn up the heat for a few minutes, and let the liquid bubble away until only a little sauce is left. Put the carrots onto a plate, and pour the sauce over them.

FROZEN CARROTS OR MIXED VEGETABLES

Allow 3–4 oz (75–100g) per serving. Cook in boiling, salted water as directed on the packet, and serve as above.

CAULIFLOWER

Most cauliflowers are too large for one person, but they can be cut in half and the remainder kept in the fridge for use in the next few days. Try not to bruise the florets when cutting them, as they will discolour easily. Very small caulis and packets of cauliflower florets are sold in some supermarkets.

Allow 3–4 florets per serving.

Trim off tough stem and outer leaves. The cauli can either be left whole or divided into florets. Wash thoroughly. Cook in boiling, salted water for 5 to 15 minutes, according to size, until just tender. Drain well. Serve hot, with a knob of butter, a spoonful of soured cream, or white sauce (see page 231). For cauliflower cheese, see page 46.

FROZEN CAULIFLOWER
Allow 4–6 oz (100–150g) per serving. Cook as directed on the packet and serve as above.

CAULIFLOWER SAVOURY
Serves 2–4

Makes a light supper dish for two, or a lovely tasty vegetable accompaniment with cold meat for four people. You can substitute broccoli for the cauliflower and add any other extra vegetables you may have available if you like.

Preparation and cooking time: 35–40 minutes.

1 lb (500g) cauliflower (or more or less according to appetite)
3–4 rashers of streaky bacon
1 onion
1 tbsp oil (for frying)
1 heaped tbsp flour or cornflour
½ pt (300ml) milk
4 oz (100g) grated cheese
1–2 tbsp fresh breadcrumbs
Salt, black pepper, paprika or cayenne pepper

Heat the oven to 400°F/200°C/Gas Mark 6–7. Grease well a 2½ pt (1.5 litre) oven-proof dish.

Break the cauliflower into florets, and slice any extra vegetables you are using. Chop the bacon, peel and slice the onion and fry them together in the oil over a moderate heat for 4 to 5 minutes, until the bacon is cooked. Mix in the flour or cornflour and gradually stir in the milk, cooking it gently until the sauce thickens. Mix in three-quarters of the cheese and season to taste.

Put the cauliflower and any extra vegetables into the greased dish. Pour the hot sauce over, mix the remaining cheese with the breadcrumbs and scatter over the top of the sauce. Bake in the hot oven for 10 to 15 minutes, until crisp and golden brown on top.

CELERIAC

4. Celeriac

The root of a variety of celery, celeriac is one of the more unusual vegetables now available in good greengrocers and larger supermarkets.

Allow 4–8 oz (100–225g) per person.

Peel fairly thickly, and cut into evenly-sized chunks. Put into a saucepan with boiling water, and cook for 30 to 40 minutes. Drain well. Serve with butter, or mash with a potato masher, fork or whisk, with a little butter and top of the milk. Season with salt and pepper.

CELERY

Most popular eaten raw, with cheese, or chopped up in a salad. It can be cooked and served as a hot vegetable; the tougher outer stems can be used for cooking, leaving the tender inner stems to be eaten raw.

Allow 3–4 stalks of celery per serving.

Trim the celery stalk. Divide it into separate stems. Wash each stem well and scrape off any stringy bits with a knife. The celery is now ready to eat raw. To cook, chop the celery into 1 in (2.5cm) lengths. Put it into a saucepan, with boiling, salted water, and cook for 10 minutes, until just tender. Drain well, serve with a knob of butter, or put into a greased, oven-proof dish, top with 1–2 oz (25–50g) grated cheese, and brown under a hot grill.

CHICORY

This can be used raw in salads, or cooked carefully in water and butter, and served hot.

Allow 6–8 oz (175–225g/one head) per serving.

5. Chicory

Remove any damaged outer leaves and trim the stalk. With a pointed vegetable knife, cut a cone-shaped core out of the base, to ensure even cooking and reduce bitterness. Wash in cold water. Put the chicory into a saucepan with a knob of butter, 2–3 tbsp water and a pinch of salt. Cook gently for about 20 minutes, until just tender, making sure that all the liquid does not disappear. Serve with melted butter.

CHINESE LEAVES

These can be used raw in salads. Keep the Chinese leaves in a polythene bag in the fridge to keep them crisp until you want to use them.

Allow ¼–½ small cabbage per serving.

Trim off any spoiled leaves and stalks. Shred finely. Wash and drain well (in a salad shaker or a clean tea-towel). Use in salad with any other salad vegetables (cucumber, tomato, cress, spring onions, raddish etc.) and a vinaigrette dressing (2 tbsp oil, 1 tsp vinegar, pinch of salt, pepper and sugar, all mixed well together).

COURGETTES

These are baby marrows. They are very quick and easy to prepare, and are quite economical as there is almost no waste with them.

Allow 1 or 2 courgettes (4–6 oz/100–175g) per serving, according to size.

Top and tail very tiny courgettes, and leave them whole. Slice larger ones into rings (½–1 in/1.25–2.5cm) or large dice. Wash well.

BOILED

Prepare the courgettes as above. Boil them gently in salted water for 2 to 5 minutes, until just tender. Drain them very well, as they tend to be a bit watery. (You can get them really dry by shaking them in the pan over a very low heat for a moment.) Serve topped with a knob of butter, or tip them into a greased, oven-proof dish and top with 1 oz (25g) grated cheese, and brown under a hot grill. Courgettes can also be served with white, cheese or parsley sauce.

FRIED

Prepare the courgettes as above. Wash and drain them well and dry on kitchen paper. Melt a little cooking oil and butter in a frying pan, add the courgettes and fry gently for a few minutes, until tender. Drain on kitchen paper. Serve hot.

PIPERADE-STUFFED COURGETTES   *Serves 1 or 2*

Use good-sized, even-shaped courgettes for this dish, which can be served as a starter for two or a generous main course for one person.

Preparation and cooking time: 30–35 minutes.

1–2 medium-size courgettes
Salt and pepper
½ small onion
½ small green or red pepper
1–2 tomatoes, fresh or canned
1 tbsp vegetable oil
Pinch of garlic powder
2 eggs
Few sprigs of fresh parsley

Trim and wash the courgettes, and cook whole in gently boiling salted water for 6 to 7 minutes, until just soft (test by pricking with a fork). Drain the courgettes, and leave in the saucepan with the lid on while you prepare the piperade.

Make the piperade: Peel and slice the onion. Wash, core and chop the pepper. Wash and chop the tomatoes. Heat the oil in a saucepan and cook the onion and pepper over a medium heat, stirring well, for about 4 to 5 minutes, until soft. Add the chopped tomatoes, garlic, salt and pepper, and stir. Continue to cook gently over a low heat, stirring occasionally, for about 15 minutes, to make a thick saucy mixture.

Break the eggs into a small basin and lightly beat them with a fork, ready to cook.

Remove the courgettes from the pan, split them in half lengthways and hollow out the seedy centre part, leaving a thick courgette shell. Put them on a serving dish and keep them warm while cooking the egg.

Pour the beaten egg into the vegetable mixture, stirring hard with a wooden spoon over a low heat until the eggs are just setting (do not over-cook or the eggs will go hard instead of soft and creamy). Spoon the filling into the prepared courgette halves. Eat hot or cold as preferred.

CUCUMBER

Most widely used as a salad vegetable and eaten raw, although it can be cut in chunks and added to casseroles, or cooked in the same way as courgettes or celery. Cucumbers are usually bought *whole, or cut in half.* They keep best in the fridge, wrapped in a polythene bag.

Wash the cucumber. Peel thinly (if you wish) or leave unpeeled. Cut into thin slices and use with salad, or munch a chunk like an apple, with a ploughman's lunch.

LEEKS

These must be thoroughly washed or they will taste gritty.

Allow 1 or 2 leeks per serving, according to size and appetite.

Cut off the roots and the tough green part, just leaving any green that looks appetising. Slit down one side and rinse well in cold, running water to get rid of all the soil and grit – this is a bit fiddly and it will take a few minutes to get them thoroughly clean. Leave them whole, or cut them into shorter lengths if they are very large, or into rings.

Cook in a very little boiling, salted water for 5 to 10 minutes, according to size, or sauté in a little oil or butter for a few minutes. Drain well. Serve at once, or put into a greased oven-proof dish, cover with 1 oz (25g) grated cheese and brown under a hot grill or serve with white sauce which can be prepared while the leeks are cooking.

LETTUCE

Cheapest and best in spring and summer, when various kinds are available. Choose a lettuce that looks crisp and firm, with a solid heart; if it looks limp and flabby it is old and stale. Lettuce will keep for a few days in a polythene bag or a box in the fridge, but goes slimy if left too long, so buy *a small lettuce* unless you're going to eat a lot of salad.

Cut off the stalk and discard any brown or battered leaves. Pull the leaves off the stem and wash separately in cold, running water. Dry thoroughly in a salad shaker or clean tea-towel. Put into a polythene bag or box in the fridge if not using immediately, to keep it crisp. Serve as a basic green salad or as a garnish with bread rolls, cheese or cold meat, or as a side salad with hot dishes (alone or with a French dressing).

MARROW

Very cheap when in season, during the autumn. *A small marrow* will serve three or four people as a vegetable with meat or fish, or can be stuffed with meat or rice to make a dinner or supper dish.

Wash the marrow in cold water. Peel thinly. Cut into 1 in (2.5cm) rings or cubes, according to size. Boil gently in salted water for 3 to 6 minutes, until just tender. Drain very well, as marrow can be a bit watery. (You can get the pieces really dry by shaking them in the pan over a very low heat for a few moments.) Serve topped with a knob of butter, or tip the pieces into a greased oven-proof dish and top with 1 oz (25g) grated cheese, and brown under a hot grill. Marrow can also be served with white, cheese or parsley sauce.

MUSHROOMS

Buy in small amounts, *2 oz (50g)*, so that they can be eaten fresh. Fresh mushrooms are pale-coloured and look plump and firm; older ones look dried-up and brownish. Keep mushrooms in the fridge. Mushrooms can be fried or grilled with bacon, sausages, chops or steaks. Add them to casseroles or stews or make a tasty snack by cooking them in butter and garlic and serving on toast (see page 59).

Allow 2–3 mushrooms each, according to size, or 1–2 oz (25–50g).

FRIED

Wash the mushrooms in cold water. Leave them whole or slice large ones if you wish. Fry them gently in a little butter and oil for a few minutes, until soft. They can be put in the frying pan with bacon or sausages, or cooked alone in a smaller saucepan.

GRILLED

Put a small knob of butter in each mushroom and grill them for a few minutes in the base of the grill pan. If you are grilling them with bacon, sausages or chops put them under the grill rack; the juice from the meat and mushrooms makes a tasty sauce.

SAVOURY MUSHROOM PIE
Serves 1

A tasty potato-topped dinner or supper dish. The pie can be made in advance and kept in the fridge or frozen until needed. It is then best to heat it through thoroughly in a moderate oven (350°F/180°C/Gas Mark 4–5) for 10 to 15 minutes until hot and golden brown on top.

Preparation and cooking time: 45 minutes.

2 medium-size potatoes (more or less according to appetite)
Salt and pepper
1 onion
1 clove of garlic or ¼ tsp garlic powder
1 stick of celery
4 oz (100g) mushrooms
½ oz (12g) butter
1 oz (25g) grated Cheddar or Edam cheese
1 tbsp vegetable oil
1 tsp flour or cornflour
½ cup milk
2 tbsp cashew nuts or pinenut kernels
½ tsp mixed herbs
Few sprigs of parsley
½ tsp lemon juice
1 tomato, sliced (for decoration)

Peel the potatoes, cut them into thick slices and cook in boiling salted water for 8 to 10 minutes until the potatoes feel soft when tested with a knife.

Peel and slice the onion and fresh garlic. Wash and chop the celery. Wash and slice the mushrooms.

Drain the potatoes when cooked, then mash with a potato masher or fork and wooden spoon. Beat in the butter and grated cheese and season with salt and pepper. Leave in the pan with the lid on.

Heat the oil in a saucepan over a medium heat and fry the onion, celery and garlic gently for 4 to 5 minutes until soft. Add the mushrooms and continue to cook gently for 3 to 4 minutes, stirring occasionally.

Mix the flour or cornflour to a smooth paste with 1 tbsp of the milk, stir in the rest of the milk and pour it all into the mushroom mixture, stirring over a low heat until the sauce thickens. Add the nuts, herbs and washed, scissor-snipped parsley, lemon juice, salt and pepper and simmer for a further 2 to 3 minutes, stirring gently.

Put the vegetable mixture into an individual pie dish. Top with the cheeesy potato and fork the top decoratively. Garnish with the tomato slices and brown under a hot grill until golden brown.

OKRA

6. Okra

Known as Ladies' Fingers, okra consists of curved seed pods. It can be served as a vegetable with meat or curry, or fried with tomatoes, onions and spices with rice as a supper dish.

Allow 2 oz (50g) per serving.

Top and tail the okra. Wash it in cold water. Put 1–2 tbsp cooking oil in a pan, add the okra and cook gently, stirring occasionally for 15 to 20 minutes, until the okra feels tender when tested with a pointed knife. It should have a slightly glutinous texture.

OKRA WITH TOMATO
1 very generous helping

Try this more unusual vegetable as a light lunch or supper dish, served with rice or warm pitta bread, or use it as a tasty accompaniment to roasts or burgers.

Preparation and cooking time: 35–45 minutes.

4 oz (100g) fresh okra
1 small onion
1 clove of garlic or ¼ tsp garlic granules
1–2 tomatoes, fresh or canned
1–2 tbsp vegetable oil
1 tsp tomato purée or ketchup
Salt and pepper
¼ tsp sugar
½ tsp mixed herbs or ground coriander
1 tsp lemon juice
½ cup (approx.) cold water or juice from canned tomatoes

Top and tail the okra, rinse in cold water. Peel and slice the onion. Peel and finely chop the fresh garlic. Wash and chop the fresh tomatoes.

Heat the oil in a pan over a moderate heat, and fry the onion and garlic gently for 3 to 4 minutes, until softened but not browned. Add the okra, and continue to cook gently for a further 4 to 5 minutes, until beginning to soften.

Add the chopped tomatoes, tomato purée or ketchup, salt, pepper, sugar, herbs and lemon juice. Add about ½ cup of water or tomato juice, just enough to half cover the vegetables in the pan, and simmer for about 20 to 30 minutes, until the okra is tender.

Taste the sauce and adjust the seasoning if necessary. Serve hot or cold (but I prefer it hot).

ONIONS

The best way to peel onions without crying is to cut off their tops and tails and then peel off their skins with a vegetable knife under cold running water.

To chop onions evenly, peel them under cold water, then slice them downwards vertically into evenly-sized rings. If you want finely-chopped onion pieces, slice the rings through again horizontally.

ROAST ONION

Allow 1 medium or large onion per person. Spanish onions are good for roasting. Top, tail and peel the onion. Heat a little oil or fat in a roasting tin (400°F/200°C/Gas Mark 6). When hot (3 to 5 minutes) place the onion carefully in the hot fat – it will spit, beware! Roast for 45 minutes to 1 hour. Onions are delicious roasted with a joint of meat and roast potatoes.

BAKED ONION

Allow 1 large onion per person. Spanish onions are the best. Rinse the onion, top and tail it, but do not peel it. Put it in a tin or baking dish, and bake for 45 minutes to 1 hour (400°F/200°C/Gas Mark 6). Slit and serve with butter.

BOILED ONION

Allow 1 medium onion per person. Top, tail and peel the onion. Put it in a pan of boiling water and simmer for 20 to 30 minutes, according to its size, until tender.

FRIED ONION

Allow 1 onion per person. Top, tail and peel the onion and slice into rings. Fry them gently in a saucepan with a little oil and butter, for 5 to 10 minutes, until soft and golden, stirring occasionally. Delicious with liver and bacon.

PARSNIPS

These are very tasty and can be roasted on their own, or with roast potatoes.

Allow 1 parsnip per person if small, or a large parsnip will cut into 5 or 6 pieces.

Parsnips are cooked in the same way as roast potatoes (see page 108), but do not cut them into too small pieces or they get too crispy. If you peel them before you are ready to cook them, keep them covered in a pan of cold water, as they go brown very quickly. (If this should happen, the parsnips will still be all right to cook, they will just look a bit speckled.)

PEAS

Most commonly available tinned or frozen nowadays. But fresh peas are a lovely treat in the summer, so try some.

Allow 8 oz (225g) peas in the pod per serving.

Shell the peas and remove any maggotty ones. Boil them gently in salted water, with a sprig of mint if possible, for 5 to 10 minutes. Drain them well, remove the mint and serve with a sprinkle of sugar and a knob of butter.

FROZEN PEAS

Allow 3–4 oz (75–100g) per serving. Cook as directed on the packet.

MANGETOUT PEAS OR SUGAR SNAP PEAS

Becoming widely available in supermarkets. Quite expensive but can be bought in small amounts and you eat the lot, including the pods!

Allow approximately 4 oz (100g) per serving.

Top and tail the peas with a vegetable knife or a pair of scissors. Wash them and leave them whole. Put them into a pan of boiling, salted water and boil for 2 to 3 minutes. They are slightly crumbly when cooked. Serve hot with a knob of butter.

GREEN, RED OR YELLOW PEPPERS

Use raw in a green salad, or cook, filled with rice or meat stuffing, for a lunch or supper dish (see below), or stewed in oil with tomatoes and garlic as a filling vegetable dish. *Peppers can be bought singly.* Choose crisp, firm-looking ones and store them in the fridge to keep them fresh.

Rinse them in cold water, cut off the top, scoop out the core and seeds. Cut into rings or chunks and use in salad or as a garnish.

STUFFED PEPPERS
Serves 1

Green peppers are available in the shops all year round, but their price varies considerably, so shop around for a 'good buy'. As with avocados, peppers come from different countries and the price will vary during the year. Serve with a side salad and brown crusty bread.

Preparation and cooking time: 45 minutes.

1 small onion
1 tbsp oil (for frying)
4 oz (100g) minced beef
1 small tomato
1 tsp tomato purée (or ketchup)
½ stock cube
½ cup boiling water
Salt and pepper
Pinch of herbs
1 tbsp raw rice or 2 tbsp cooked rice if you have any left-over
    (optional)
1–2 green peppers

Peel and chop the onion. Heat the oil in a saucepan. Add the onion and fry gently for a few minutes, until soft. Add the minced beef to the onion, and continue to fry for 2 to 3 minutes, stirring frequently. Wash and chop the tomato. Add it to the meat in the pan, with the tomato purée (or ketchup).

Dissolve the stock cube in the boiling water. Add it to the meat, with the salt, pepper and herbs. Continue simmering over a moderate heat. Stir in the washed raw rice and leave to simmer for 15 to 20 minutes, stirring occasionally. The stock should be almost completely absorbed. Cut the tops off the peppers. Remove the seeds and wash the peppers.

Grease an oven-proof dish. Remove the meat mixture from the heat. Strain off any excess liquid (the mixture wants to be damp but not swimming in gravy). If you are using left-over cooked rice, mix it in with the meat mixture. Fill the peppers with the meat mixture and put them into the greased oven-proof dish. Bake in a hot oven (350°F/180°C/Gas Mark 4–5) for 30 minutes.

BOILED POTATOES

Try to select potatoes of the same size to cook together, or cut large potatoes into evenly-sized pieces, so that all the potatoes will be cooked at the same time. (Very big potatoes will go soggy on the outside before the inside is cooked if left whole.) Do not let the water boil too fast, or the potatoes will tend to break up.

Allow 2–4 potato pieces per person.

Peel the potatoes as thinly as you can. Dig out any eyes or any black bits with as little waste as possible. Put them in a saucepan. Cover with hot water and add a pinch of salt. Bring to the boil, then lower the heat and simmer for 15 to 20 minutes, until they feel just soft when tested with a knife. Drain and serve hot.

MASHED POTATOES

The best way of serving boiled potatoes that have broken up during cooking. Prepare the boiled potatoes as described above. (If you are in a hurry, cut the potatoes into thick slices and cook for less time, about 10 minutes.) When they are cooked, drain the potatoes well. Mash them with a fork or masher until fluffy, then heap onto a serving dish.

CREAMED POTATOES

Prepare mashed potatoes as above. When they are really fluffy beat in a knob of butter and a little top of the milk. Fork into a heap on a serving dish and top with a dab of butter.

POTATO CASTLES

Prepare creamed potatoes as above. Grease a flat baking tin or an oven-proof plate, and pile the potatoes onto it, in 2 or 3 evenly-sized heaps. Fork them into castles, top with a bit of butter and either brown under the grill for a minute or two, or put them into a hot oven (400°F/200°C/Gas Mark 6) for 5 to 10 minutes, until crisp and golden brown.

CHEESY POTATOES

Prepare creamed potatoes as above, beating 1–2 oz (25–50g) grated cheese into the potatoes with the butter. Pile the potatoes into a greased oven-proof dish, fork down evenly and top with a little grated cheese. Brown under a hot grill for a minute or two, or put into a hot oven (400°F/200°C/Gas Mark 6) for 5 to 10 minutes, until golden.

ROAST POTATOES

These can be cooked around the joint if you are cooking a roast dinner, or in a baking tin, with a little hot fat, to cook on their own. *Allow 2–4 potato pieces per person.*

Peel the potatoes and cut them into evenly-sized pieces. Put them in a saucepan of hot water, bring to the boil and simmer for 2 to 3 minutes. Put a little fat in a roasting tin. (Use lard, margarine, dripping or oil. Do not use butter on its own as it burns and goes brown.) Heat the tin in the oven (400–425°F/200–220°C/Gas Mark 6–7). Drain the potatoes and shake them in the pan over the heat for a moment to dry them. Put the potatoes into the hot roasting tin, but be careful that the hot fat does not spit and burn you. Roast for 45 to 60 minutes, according to size, until crisp and golden brown.

NEW POTATOES

Lovely and easy – no peeling! *Allow 3–6 new potatoes, according to size and appetite.*

Wash the potatoes well under running water and scrub them with a pan scrubber or a brush. If you prefer, scrape with a vegetable knife also. Put them in a pan, cover them with boiling water, add salt and a sprig of mint. Bring to the boil and simmer for 15 to 20 minutes, until tender. Drain well, tip onto a plate and top with a little butter.

SAUTÉ POTATOES

A way of using up left-over boiled or roast potatoes. Alternatively potatoes can be boiled specially, and then sautéed when they have gone cold. *Allow approximately 3–4 cold cooked potato pieces, according to appetite.*

Slice the potatoes thinly. Heat a little oil and butter in a frying pan. Add the potato slices and fry them gently for 5 minutes, until crisp and golden, turning frequently with a fish slice or spatula.

ONION SAUTÉ POTATOES

Peel and thinly slice a small onion. Fry the onion in a frying pan with a little oil and butter until it is just soft, then add the cold, sliced potatoes and fry as above until crisp and delicious. Serve at once.

JACKET SPUDS

These can be served as an accompaniment to meat or fish or made into a meal on their own, with any one of a number of fillings heaped on top of them. *Allow 1 medium – large potato per person.*

Choose potatoes that do not have any mouldy-looking patches on the skin. Remember that very large potatoes will take longer to cook, so if you're hungry it's better to cook 2 medium-sized spuds. Wash and scrub the potato. Prick it

several times with a fork. For quicker c........g, spear
potatoes onto a metal skewer or potato baker.

TRADITIONAL WAY
Put the potato into the oven (400°F/200°C/Gas Mark 6) for 1
to 1½ hours according to size. The skin should be crisp and
the inside soft and fluffy when ready. If you prefer softer
skin, or don't want to risk the potato bursting all over the
oven, wrap the spud loosely in a piece of cooking foil before
putting it into the oven.

QUICKER WAY
Put the potato into a saucepan, cover with hot water, bring to
the boil and cook for 5 to 10 minutes according to size. Drain
it carefully, lift the potato out with a cloth, and put into a hot
oven (400°F/200°C/Gas Mark 6) for 30 to 60 minutes,
according to size, until it feels soft.

If you are cooking a casserole in the oven at a lower
temperature, put the potato in the oven with it, and allow
extra cooking time.

BAKED STUFFED POTATO
Useful to serve with cold meat or with steak, as it can be
prepared in advance and heated up at the last minute.

Scrub and bake a largish jacket potato as described above.
When the potato is soft, remove from the oven, and cut it
carefully in half lengthways. Scoop the soft potato into a
bowl, and mash with a fork, adding ½ oz (12g) butter and
½ oz (12g) grated cheese. Pile the filling back into the skin
again and fork down evenly. Place on a baking tin or oven-
proof plate, sprinkle a little grated cheese on top, and either
brown under the hot grill for a few minutes, or put into a hot
oven (400°F/200°C/Gas Mark 6) for 5 to 10 minutes, until
browned.

A FEW FILLINGS

Prepare and cook the jacket spuds. When soft, put them onto a plate, split open and top with your chosen filling and a knob of butter.

Cheese
1–2 oz (25–50g) grated cheese.

Cheese and Onion
1 small finely-sliced onion and 1–2 oz (25–50g) grated cheese.

Cheese and Pickle
1–2 oz (25–50g) grated cheese and 1 tsp pickle or chutney.

Cottage Cheese
2–3 tbsp cottage cheese (plain or with chives, pineapple, etc.).

Baked Beans
Heat a small tin of baked beans and pour over the potato.

Bolognese
Top with Bolognese sauce (see page 210). This is a good way of using up any extra sauce left over from Spaghetti Bolognese.

Bacon
Chop 1–2 rashers of bacon into pieces. Fry them for a few minutes, until crisp, then pour over the potato.

Egg
Top with 1–2 fried eggs, a scrambled egg or an omelette.

Curry
Top with any left-over curry sauce, heated gently in a saucepan until piping hot.

SCALLOPED POTATOES

Tasty and impressive-looking potatoes. Quick to prepare but they take an hour to cook, so they can be put in the oven and left while you are preparing the rest of the meal, or they can cook on a shelf above a casserole in the oven. (The potatoes need a higher temperature so put them on the top shelf and the casserole lower down.)

Allow 1–2 potatoes per person according to size and appetite.

Grease an oven-proof dish well. Peel the potatoes and slice them as thinly as possible. Put them in layers in the greased dish, sprinkling each layer with a little flour, salt and pepper. Almost cover them with ½–1 cup of milk (or milk and water). Dot with a large knob of butter. Put the dish, uncovered, in a hot oven (400°F/200°C/Gas Mark 6) for about an hour, until the potatoes are soft and most of the liquid has been absorbed. The top should be crispy.

Packets of scalloped potatoes are available in super-markets. They are more expensive than making your own, but are easy to prepare following the packet instructions.

CHIPS

If you must make your own chips do take great care. There are many good 'ready-made' frozen chips which you can buy at the supermarket, which can be cooked in the oven or shallow-fried in a little fat in an ordinary frying pan. You would be well-advised to use these when you want chips, unless you are an experienced cook and have the correct equipment for deep-fat frying. Please, please don't attempt to make chips, or indeed do any deep-fat frying, unless you have the use of a 'proper' chip pan (the electric thermostatically-controlled type preferably) and have had some previous experience of deep-fat frying under super-vision. *Allow 2–3 large potatoes per person.*

Only pour enough oil into the chip pan to cover as far as the marks on the pan, which will be no more than a quarter of the way up the pan, as the hot fat rises alarmingly when the chips or other foods are lowered into it. If the pan should catch alight, turn off the cooker and put the lid on the pan immediately. Do not move the pan or throw water over it. Follow the manufacturer's instructions carefully about using the pan, and heat the oil to the correct setting (probably about 380°F/190°C), so that it is hot and just hazing, not smoking, when you are ready to cook the chips.

Peel the potatoes, and cut them into slices ¼ in (0.5cm) thick, and cut these slices into chips. Dry the chips on a clean cloth or kitchen paper, and sprinkle with a little salt, if desired. When the fat is the correct temperature, put the chips into the chip basket and lower this carefully into the fat. Cook for 3 to 4 minutes, shaking the basket occasionally to ensure the chips are cooking evenly – don't let the fat splash onto you or the surroundings.

Remove the basket and rest it on the rim of the pan, letting the oil on the chips drip into the oil in the pan. Allow the oil in the pan to heat up again. Plunge the basket back into the oil for another minute to crisp the chips. Remove from the fat and drain as before for just a moment, then tip the hot chips onto the kitchen paper to drain. SWITCH OFF THE CHIP PAN. Serve the chips immediately. When the fat is cold, it should be strained through a fine sieve to get rid of any burnt bits or crumbs, and stored for future use, either in the chip pan or in a clean jar.

INSTANT MASH

Although more expensive then fresh potato, this makes a quick standby which saves you the trouble of peeling potatoes. The flavour and price of the different makes vary (the most expensive may not necessarily be the best), so try them out until you find one you prefer. Afterwards, it is usually more economical to buy the large size, as it keeps fresh in a container for ages. To make up the potato, follow the packet instructions. The amounts given are for rather small servings, and you may need to make extra if you're hungry. A big knob of butter (added just before serving) improves both the flavour and the appearance.

POTATO SUPPER

Serves 2 as a supper
3–4 as a vegetable

A pauper's supper dish, but a feast fit for a king when served as an accompaniment to a main meal.

Preparation and cooking time: 45–50 minutes.

1 lb (500g) boiled potatoes
4–6 oz (100–150g) strong Cheddar cheese
2 eggs
1 cup (¼ pt/150ml) milk
Salt, pepper, nutmeg, few sprigs of parsley
1 oz (25g) butter

For a supper dish:
1–2 tomatoes, sliced
1 hard-boiled egg, sliced
Small bunch of watercress

Heat the oven to 375°F/190°C/Gas Mark 5–6. Slice the cooked potatoes thinly, grate the cheese. Grease a 2½ pt/ 1 litre pie or shallow oven-proof dish well and put in a layer of potatoes, cover with half the cheese and then put another layer using up the remaining potato. Beat the eggs, stir in the milk, season with salt, pepper and nutmeg and snip in the parsley. Pour the mixture over the potatoes. Top with the remaining cheese and dot with the butter. If serving as a supper dish on its own, decorate the top with sliced tomatoes.

Cook in the hot oven for 20 to 25 minutes, until the custard is set and the top is golden and bubbly. Serve as it is for an accompaniment, or top the cooked dish with the sliced hard-boiled egg and washed watercress sprigs if eating on its own.

PUMPKIN

Generally associated with Hallowe'en, Cinderella and American Thanksgiving Day! It is available fresh in England around the end of October when it may be quite cheap. It is prepared and cooked in the same way as marrow. See page 99.

SALSIFY

A less well-known root vegetable, with soft, white flesh.
Allow 1–2 salsify roots per person.

Scrape the roots in a bowl of cold water. The roots must be kept under the cold water when being scraped, to stop discolouration. Cut them into evenly-sized rings. Cook, as soon as possible, in boiling water for 5 to 15 minutes, until tender. Drain, and serve with a knob of butter.

SPINACH

Allow 8 oz (225g) per person.

Spinach must be washed thoroughly in cold water, to get rid of all dust and grit. This will take several rinses. Remove any tough-looking leaves and stalks and cut into convenient-sized lengths (4 in/10cm). Put the spinach in a large saucepan, with no extra water, and cook over a medium heat for 7 to 10 minutes, until soft. As the spinach boils down, chop it about with a metal spoon or knife, and turn it over so that it cooks evenly, in its own juices. Drain very well, pressing the water out to get the spinach as dry as possible. Put a knob of butter in the pan with the drained spinach, and reheat for a few moments. Serve with the melted butter, seasoned well with salt and pepper.

FROZEN SPINACH

Allow 4 oz (100g) per person. Packets of frozen spinach are available all the year round in supermarkets. Cook as instructed on the packet and serve with butter as above.

SWEDE ('NEEPS' IN SCOTLAND)

Known as 'poisonous' by one member of our family, but really it is a delicious winter vegetable.

Buy a very small swede for one person, or a slightly larger one for 2 servings.

Peel thickly, so that no brown or green skin remains. Cut into ½ in (1.25cm) chunks. Cook in boiling, salted water for 15 to 20 minutes, until tender. Drain well (if you are making gravy at the same time, save the water for the gravy liquid), and mash with a fork or potato masher, adding a knob of butter and plenty of pepper.

If you wish, peel 1 or 2 carrots, cut them into rings and cook them with the swede, mashing the two vegetables together with butter as above, or just mix the two together without mashing.

SWEETCORN

Frozen corn-on-the-cob is available all the year round. Cook as directed on the packet. Fresh cobs are in the shops from August to October, although imported sweetcorn is sometimes available at other times.

Cut off the stalk, remove the leaves and silky threads – this may be a bit fiddly, but try and pull all the threads off. Put the sweetcorn into a large pan of boiling, unsalted water, and simmer for 8 to 10 minutes, until the kernels are tender. Drain and serve with plenty of butter by melting a little in the hot saucepan and pouring it over the cobs. Tooth picks, cocktail sticks or 2 forks will serve as corn-on-the-cob holders.

SWEET POTATOES

Not directly related to ordinary potatoes. Becoming more widely available in many supermarkets. Peel, boil and purée them like creamed potatoes or cook them like roast potatoes.

TOMATOES

'Love apples' add colour and flavour to many dishes. They are used raw in salads or as a garnish, can be grilled or fried, chopped up and added to casseroles or stews, or stuffed as a supper dish. Choose firm tomatoes and keep them in the fridge for freshness. Cheaper soft tomatoes are a good buy for cooking, provided that you are going to use them straightaway.

Wash and dry the tomatoes, cut them into slices or quarters to use in a salad or as a garnish. Tomatoes are easy to cut or slice thinly if you use a bread knife or a vegetable knife with a serrated edge. The skin will then cut more easily without the inside squidging out.

GRILLED

Cut them in half, dot with butter and grill for 3 to 5 minutes. Alternatively, put them in the grill pan under the grid when grilling sausages, bacon, chops or steak, as the tomatoes will then cook with the meat.

FRIED

Cut the tomatoes in half and fry them in a little oil or fat, on both sides, over a medium heat, for a few minutes until soft. Serve with bacon and sausages, or place on a slice of toast or fried bread.

BAKED

Cut a cross in the top of any small or medium-sized tomatoes and halve any large ones. Put them into a greased, oven-proof dish or tin, with a knob of butter on top. Bake for 10 to 15 minutes (350°F/180°C/Gas Mark 4), until soft.

TURNIPS

Small white root vegetables, not to be confused with swedes.

Allow ½–2 turnips per serving, according to size and appetite.

Peel the turnips thickly. Leave small ones whole but cut large turnips in half or quarters. Cook them in boiling, salted water for 10 minutes, until soft. Drain them well. Return the turnips to the pan and shake over a low heat for a few moments to dry them out. Serve with a knob of butter.

Turnips can also be served with 1 or 2 diced carrots. Just peel them and cut them into large dice, mix them with the carrots and boil them together for 5 to 10 minutes. Drain and dry as above.

PURÉE

Peel the turnips and cut them into chunks. Cook them in boiling water for 5 to 10 minutes, until soft. Drain well, and dry as above. Mash with a fork or potato masher, with a knob of butter and some pepper.

BOILED RICE

A good quick standby, which saves peeling potatoes. Long grain, or Patna type, rice is used for savoury rice; the smaller, round grain type is used for puddings. Brown rice is also used for savoury dishes, but takes longer to cook. Rice is cheaper to buy in a large packet, and keeps for ages if decanted into a jar or plastic container. You can buy prepared and 'easy cook' rice of several types in the supermarkets, which must be cooked exactly as described on the packet. This type of rice is very good and easy to cook, but is usually more expensive than plain, long grain rice.

METHOD ONE

I prefer to use this method, as I tend to let the pan boil dry with the alternative method! However, you do need a largish pan and it's a bit steamy as the rice must be cooked without the lid on, otherwise it boils over.

Preparation and cooking time: 13 minutes.

½ cup (3 oz/75g) long grain rice – white or brown
½ tsp salt

Wash the rice well to get rid of the starch (put it into a saucepan and slosh it around in several rinses of cold water). Put the rice into a largish pan. Fill the pan two-thirds full of boiling water. Add the salt. Bring back to the boil and boil gently for 10 to 12 minutes for white rice, 20 to 25 minutes for brown rice, until the rice is cooked but still firm. Do not overcook or it will go sticky and puddingy. Drain well. Fluff with a fork and serve.

METHOD TWO
Be careful that the rice doesn't boil dry.

Preparation and cooking time: 13–16 minutes.

½ cup (3 oz/75g) long grain white rice
1 tsp oil or small knob of butter
1 cup boiling water
Pinch of salt

Wash the rice as in method one. Put the oil or butter in a smallish saucepan and heat gently. Then add the rice, stirring all the time, to coat each grain. Add the boiling water and a pinch of salt, bring up to simmering point and stir. Put on the lid and leave the rice to simmer over a very gentle heat for 12 to 15 minutes. Test to see if the rice is cooked: all the liquid should be absorbed and the rice should be cooked but not soggy. Lightly fluff with a fork and serve.

FRIED RICE

Serves 1

You can either use up left-over boiled rice (I always cook too much) or cook some specially.

Preparation and cooking time: 15 minutes (plus 15 minutes if you have to boil the rice first).

1 cup cooked boiled rice (use ½ cup raw rice)
½ onion or 1 spring onion
½ slice cooked, chopped ham (optional)
1 tbsp cooking oil
1 tbsp frozen peas and/or sweetcorn (optional)

Cook the rice if necessary (see page 118). Peel and chop the onion, or wash and chop the spring onion. Chop the ham. Heat the oil in a frying pan over a medium heat. Add the chopped onion and fry, turning frequently, until soft. Add the cooked rice, and fry for 4 to 5 minutes, stirring all the time. Add the frozen peas (still frozen; they will defrost in the pan), sweetcorn and ham, and cook for a further 2 to 3 minutes, stirring all the time, until it is all heated through.

You can make this more substantial by adding more vegetables and chopped cooked meat (ham, salami, garlic sausage, etc.) if you wish.

CHINESEY FRIED RICE

Serves 2 or more

Serve plain as an accompaniment or mixed with lots of extras to make a main meal. If serving as an accompaniment, you can omit the egg and just stir in a few vegetables to add a bit of colour to the dish. It's a good way of using up all the little bits left in the fridge, as the amounts used can vary according to availability.

Preparation and cooking time: 20 minutes.

1 egg
½ small onion or 3–4 spring onions

1 clove of garlic or ½ tsp ground garlic
2 tbsp (approx.) vegetable oil
2 cups cooked rice (or cook 1 cup (4 oz/100g) dry rice)
1 tbsp soy sauce
Salt and pepper
Few sprigs of fresh herbs – parsley, chives, mint, tarragon, etc.

Extras:
2 oz (50g) diced cooked ham, chicken or turkey
2 oz (50g) cooked, peeled prawns
Few mushrooms, sliced
2 tbsp frozen peas
2 tbsp canned or frozen sweetcorn
2 tbsp canned bamboo shoots, sliced
2 tbsp cashew nuts or pine kernels

Beat the egg in a small basin. Peel and finely chop the onion and fresh garlic or trim, wash and chop the spring onions. Prepare the chosen extras (the peas and sweetcorn can be cooked from frozen, they will defrost in the pan).

Heat the oil in a wok or frying pan over a moderate heat, pour in the beaten egg and fry until cooked. Put the egg onto a plate and cut it into thin strips.

Add more oil to the pan and fry the chopped onion and garlic for 2 to 3 minutes, until soft. Add the chosen extras and continue stir frying for about 2 or 3 minutes until cooked. Remove with a slotted spoon and put aside.

Add a little more oil if needed, tip the rice into the pan and stir fry until the rice is hot and all the grains are separate. Stir in the soy sauce and mix well to coat the rice. Add the cooked egg and extras, and fry until everything is nice and hot. Season with salt and pepper and sprinkle with a few snipped herbs if available. Serve at once.

RISOTTO

A cheap meal if you have any 'pickings' of chicken left over. Or use a thick slice of cooked ham, chicken or turkey. It can be served with a green salad. (You don't need all the vegetables listed here; choose those you like.)

Preparation and cooking time: 35 minutes.

1 egg
1 cup rice
1 small onion
1 tbsp oil (or large knob of butter or fat)
1 stock cube and 2 cups (½ pt/300ml) boiling water
1 slice (1–2 oz/25–50g) of cooked ham, chicken or turkey
2–3 mushrooms (sliced)
1 tomato
1 tbsp frozen or canned peas
1 tbsp frozen or canned sweetcorn
Salt, pepper, Worcester sauce
1 oz (25g) grated cheese and Parmesan cheese (optional)

Hard boil the egg for 10 minutes. Wash the rice in several rinses of cold water to get rid of the starch. Peel and chop the onion finely. Heat the oil or fat in a medium saucepan or frying pan with a lid. Fry the onion for 3 to 4 minutes, until soft. Add the rice and fry, stirring well, for a further 3 minutes. Dissolve the stock cube in the boiling water. Add this to the rice, stir and leave to simmer with the lid on, stirring occasionally, for 10 to 15 minutes, until the rice is tender, and the liquid almost absorbed.

Chop the meat. Peel and chop the hard-boiled egg. Wash the sliced mushrooms. Wash and chop the tomato. Add the peas, sweetcorn, mushrooms and tomato to the rice. Cook for 2 to 3 minutes, stirring gently. Then add the chopped meat and egg, and continue stirring gently until heated right through. Season with salt, pepper and Worcester sauce. Serve with lots of grated cheese and/or Parmesan and a dash of Worcester sauce.

VEGETABLE HOT POT
Serves 1

This can be made with or without cheese, to provide a tasty dish for lunch or supper, or it can be served as a vegetable accompaniment to meat, to make a substantial meal if you're really hungry. You can either buy fresh, raw vegetables, or use up left-over vegetables. This recipe is particularly suitable for vegetarians.

Preparation and cooking time: 50 minutes.

1 small onion
1–2 oz (25–50g) cheese (optional)
2–3 potatoes
Oil and knob of butter
1–2 cups (4–8 oz/100–225g) mixed vegetables – carrots, cauliflower, leeks, celery, swede, turnip etc. Keep raw and cooked vegetables separate at this stage.
1 cup (½ small can/¼ pt/150ml) vegetable soup
Salt and pepper

Peel and slice the onion. Grate the cheese. Peel the potatoes and cut them into thick slices (¼ in/0.5cm). Heat the oil and butter in a saucepan over a moderate heat, and fry the onion for 2 to 3 minutes, until soft. Add the raw vegetables (not the potatoes) and continue to fry gently for a few minutes. Stir in the soup. Bring to the boil, and then lower the heat and simmer gently for 5 to 10 minutes, until the vegetables are tender, adding any cooked vegetables for the last 2 to 3 minutes to heat them through.

Meanwhile partly cook the sliced potatoes separately in boiling, salted water for 4 to 5 minutes. Drain them. Arrange the mixed vegetables in a casserole or oven-proof dish. Stir in half the cheese and cover with the hot soup. Season with salt and pepper. Top with a thick layer of potato slices. Dot with some butter. Sprinkle with the rest of the cheese. Bake in a hot oven (400°F/200°C/Gas Mark 6–7) for 15 to 20 minutes, until the top is golden brown. Serve hot.

GENERAL VEGETABLE SOUP

Serves 4 or more

Makes a good, filling 'lunch or supper' soup, using any mixture of fresh vegetables you have to hand, adding left-over cooked vegetables when the soup is nearly cooked. For a truly vegetarian soup, use only vegetable stock and omit bacon or any gravies made from meat juices.

Preparation and cooking time: 1¼–1½ hours.

2–3 onions
1–2 cloves of garlic or ¼–½ tsp garlic paste or powder

Choose a selection of vegetables – you don't need everything!
1–2 leeks
2 large carrots
1 large potato
3–4 sticks of celery
1 small turnip or half a small swede
1 small parsnip
Few florets of cauliflower
1–2 courgettes or piece of marrow
2–4 tomatoes (use up the squashy ones)
Handful of mushrooms
Any cooked left-over vegetables – peas, carrot, courgette,
 sweetcorn, etc.
2–3 rashers of bacon
2 tbsp vegetable oil (for frying)
1 can tomatoes (optional, use a little less stock)
2 pints (1.25 litres) approx. vegetable or meat stock (home-
 made or use 2–3 stock cubes, adding left-over gravy to the
 liquid)
1–2 tsp mixed herbs (fresh or dried)
Salt and pepper
Dash of tabasco sauce
Handful of fresh parsley and/or chives

Peel and wash the chosen vegetables and slice or cut them into ½ in (1 cm) dice according to type. Peel the marrow but leave the skin on the courgettes. Cut the fresh tomatoes into quarters. Rinse and slice any large mushrooms, leave small ones whole. De-rind and chop the bacon.

Heat the oil in a large saucepan over a moderate heat, and fry the sliced onion, chopped garlic and bacon for 4 to 5 minutes until the onion is softened but not brown, and the bacon is just crisp.

Add the prepared chosen root vegetables (leeks, carrots, potato, celery, turnip, swede and parsnip) and fry for a further 4 to 5 minutes, turning them over gently in the hot oil. Add the canned tomatoes, pour on the stock and gravy, add the herbs, stir well and bring to the boil, then reduce the heat and simmer with the lid on for 20 to 30 minutes, until the vegetables are soft.

Add the remaining fresh vegetables (cauliflower florets, courgettes, marrow, tomatoes, mushrooms) and continue to simmer for a further 15 minutes, adding the left-over cooked vegetables for the last 10 minutes of cooking time.

Season well with salt, pepper and a dash of tabasco. Sprinkle with fresh snipped parsley or chives if available and serve nice and hot.

VEGETABLE CURRY
Serves 1

You can use either fresh raw vegetables, left-over cooked vegetables, frozen vegetables (sold for stews or casseroles), or a mixture of them all. Serve with boiled rice.

Preparation and cooking time: 50 minutes.

1 small onion
2 cups (8 oz/225g) mixed vegetables: carrots, cauliflower, potatoes, celery, swede, turnip, etc. Keep the raw and cooked vegetables separate at this stage if you are using both.
Little oil for frying
1–2 tsp curry powder (or to taste)
½ tsp paprika pepper
1 tsp tomato purée (or ketchup)
1 tsp apricot jam (or redcurrant jelly)
½ tsp lemon juice
1 cup (¼ pt/150ml) milk (or milk and water)
1 tbsp sultanas (or raisins)
1 egg (optional)

Peel and chop the onion. Wash and prepare the fresh vegetables and cut them into largish pieces. Heat the oil in a saucepan over a moderate heat and fry the onion for a few minutes, stirring occasionally, until soft. Add the curry powder and paprika, and cook, stirring as before, for 2 to 3 minutes. Stir in the tomato purée, apricot jam (or redcurrant jelly), lemon juice, milk and/or water and the sultanas (or raisins). Bring to the boil, then reduce the heat and leave to simmer with the lid on for 10 minutes.

Cook the raw or frozen vegetables, in boiling water, for 5 to 10 minutes. Drain them. Hard boil the egg in boiling water for 10 minutes. Then peel it and slice it thickly. Gently stir the vegetables into the curry sauce and simmer for a further 5 to 10 minutes, until the vegetables are completely cooked and the curry is hot. While the curry is simmering, cook the boiled rice. Garnish the curry with the hard-boiled egg.

VEGETABLE CRUMBLE

Serves 2

Use up cooked vegetables in this dish, it makes a little bit go much further!

Preparation and cooking time: 45 minutes.

Topping:

4 oz (125g) flour – wholemeal, white or a mixture
2 oz (50g) margarine or butter
2 oz (50g) grated cheese
2 oz (50g) chopped mixed or cashew nuts
2 tbsp sesame and/or pumpkin seeds (optional)
Salt

Filling:

2 onions
½ lb (250g) any mixture cooked vegetables – cauliflower, carrots, swede, etc.
1 tbsp oil for frying
1 heaped tsp flour or cornflour
1 cup (¼ pt/150ml) boiling water with 1 stock cube or 1 cup (¼ pt/150ml) gravy
Salt and pepper
Dash of tabasco or Worcester sauce, shake cayenne pepper

1–2 tomatoes, thinly sliced

Heat the oven to 375°F/190°C/Gas Mark 5–6.

Make the topping: Rub the flour and fat together with your fingertips until it looks like breadcrumbs (or process in a mixer if you have one). Add the cheese, nuts, seeds (if used) and salt. Mix well.

Make the filling: Peel and thinly slice the onions. Slice the cooked vegetables thickly. Put the oil into a pan over a moderate heat, and fry the onion gently for 4 to 5 minutes, until soft. Stir in the prepared vegetables and heat through. Mix the flour or cornflour with a tbsp cold water to make a runny paste. Crumble in the stock cube (if used), then stir in the boiling water or heated gravy. Stir the sauce into the vegetable mixture and cook over a low heat for 2 to 3 minutes until the sauce thickens. Season to taste.

Pour the vegetable mixture into a 2 pt (1.25 litre) deep pie dish, top with the crumble mixture and smooth over with a fork. Decorate with the sliced tomatoes and bake in the hot oven for 15 to 20 minutes until the top is nicely browned.

RATATOUILLE   *Serves 2*

'Ratts', as this is called by one member of our family, is really a delicious vegetable mixture with a Mediterranean taste. The best and traditional flavour is obtained by using a good olive oil, but any vegetable oil can be used and is generally cheaper.

Because you need a mixture of vegetables it is more economical to make a larger amount, so if you occasionally entertain, why not double the quantity given in this recipe and feed some of your friends? Ratatouille can be eaten cold or hot and, if you have access to a freezer, it freezes well in individual plastic containers. It can accompany a main meal or be eaten on its own as a light lunch, sprinkled with the traditional Greek Feta cheese.

Preparation and cooking time: 30 minutes.

1 onion
1 clove of garlic or ¼ tsp garlic granules
1 small aubergine
1–2 courgettes
½ red pepper
½ green pepper
2 tomatoes – fresh, or drained canned ones
2–3 tbsp olive or vegetable oil
Salt and pepper
1 tsp mixed herbs
Few sprigs of fresh parsley

Peel and slice the onion. Peel and chop the fresh garlic. Wash and slice the aubergine ½ in (1 cm) thick; there is no need to salt and drain the aubergine for this dish as any bitterness is masked by the general flavourings. Wash and slice the courgettes. Wash the peppers, remove the seeds and slice. Wash and thickly slice the tomatoes.

Heat the chosen oil in a medium-sized saucepan, over a moderate heat and fry the onion and garlic for 4 to 5 minutes until softened but not brown. Add the sliced aubergine, courgettes and peppers, stirring carefully into the oil, but try not to break up the vegetables. Continue frying gently and stir in the tomatoes, salt, pepper and herbs and simmer for 7 to 10 minutes, stirring occasionally, until the vegetables are cooked but not mushy.

Turn into a warmed serving dish and garnish with washed, scissor-snipped parsley and serve hot, or allow to cool and chill in the fridge if to be served cold.

BUBBLE AND SQUEAK
Serves 1

A lovely warm way of using up cold, left-over vegetables; you can, of course, cook some fresh vegetables specially if you wish.

Preparation and cooking time: 15 minutes.

3–4 cold cooked potatoes
1 cup cold cooked cabbage (or Brussels sprouts)
Little oil and a knob of butter

Slice the potatoes and chop up the cabbage or slice the sprouts. Heat the oil and butter in a frying pan over a medium heat. Put the potatoes and cabbage (or sprouts) into the frying pan and fry gently for 5 to 10 minutes, turning frequently, until the cabbage is cooked and the potatoes are golden and crispy. Serve hot with cold meat, bacon or fried eggs.

BUBBLE AND SQUEAK 'PANCAKE'

Put the boiled potato into a large bowl and mash fiercely with a potato masher. Add the cabbage and mash all together. Heat the fat in a frying pan over a moderate heat, carefully tip in the potato mixture and smooth into a large, thick pancake shape. Fry for 2 to 3 minutes, shaking the pan and loosening the 'pancake' from time to time to stop it sticking. Turn the 'pancake' over with a fish slice and cook the other side. When lovely and golden on both sides, tip it onto a warm plate and eat with cold meat and gravy, or keep it warm while you fry several eggs, then slide these on top of the 'pancake' and eat at once.

SAUTÉ OF ROAST AND BOILED VEGETABLES

Use any left-over roast vegetables (potatoes, parsnips, onions, etc.) with left-over boiled vegetables (cabbage, cauliflower, carrots, broccoli, peas, green beans, sprouts, courgettes, sweetcorn, etc.) and a peeled, thinly sliced onion.

Heat a little dripping, oil or butter in a frying pan over a moderate heat, and fry the onion slices for 2 to 3 minutes until soft. Add the sliced roast vegetables, and stir fry until the potatoes start to crisp. Stir in the remaining boiled vegetable assortment and continue to cook, turning frequently to cook evenly – adding any peas, beans, sweetcorn or other very small pieces at the last moment so that they don't get brown and too crispy. Tip onto a hot plate and serve at once. This makes a good, quick meal with cold meat, chops, bacon or sausages.

QUICK FRYING PAN SUPPER

Slice the cooked potatoes and chop up the cabbage or slice the sprouts. Heat a little fat or oil in the frying pan over a moderate heat and add one or two rashers of chopped bacon per person. Fry for a few minutes, adding some thinly sliced onion if liked. Stir in the cooked vegetables and fry until almost cooked. Make some hollows in the vegetables and slide an egg into each, allowing one or two for each person according to appetite. Put a lid on the pan and fry for 1 to 2 minutes, until the eggs are cooked to your taste. Serve on warm plates and eat at once.

HUBBLE BUBBLE

Slice the potatoes, chop up the cabbage, peel and finely slice an onion. De-rind and chop 1–2 rashers of bacon and wash and slice a few mushrooms. Heat some dripping or oil in a frying pan over a moderate heat, and fry the bacon and onion for a few minutes. Add the mushrooms, potato and cabbage and continue to fry for a few more minutes until browned. Beat an egg, and pour it over the vegetables in the pan, sprinkle with a little grated Cheddar or Parmesan cheese and cook until the egg is set; pop the pan under a hot grill for a minute to brown the top if liked. Slide onto a hot dish and eat at once.

QUICK PAN HAGGARTY

Traditionally made from raw potatoes in the North East of England. This quick method makes a really substantial snack on its own or is a tasty way of serving potatoes, especially when you want to pad out the meat! If you are only making a small amount, you will get the best results (producing a crispy outside while the middle is soft with melted cheese) using a small frying pan or omelette pan.

Peel and slice an onion and fry it in a little dripping or oil over a moderate heat for 2 to 3 minutes until softened. Slice enough boiled potatoes to suit your appetite into a bowl and stir in the softened onion. Put a layer of mixed onion and potato into the frying pan, adding a little more fat if needed, scatter on a layer of grated cheese, and repeat the layers until all the vegetables are used up, finishing with a good sprinkling of cheese. Fry gently, shaking the pan and loosening the potato with a fish slice, until the potatoes are cooked and the cheesy layers have melted; you can pop the pan under a hot grill to finish off and make a really crisp topping. Slide onto a hot dish and eat at once.

6

Bacon, Sausages and Ham

Lots of quick, but substantial snacks in this chapter. Bacon and sausages don't take long to cook and are useful when you come home hungry and want a meal in a hurry.

BACON
Streaky bacon is the cheapest, then shoulder rashers, while back and gammon are the most expensive. *Serve 1 to 2 rashers of bacon per person.* How well cooked you like your bacon is a very personal thing; I know someone who likes hers cremated! As a rough guide: cook for between 1 and 5

minutes. Tomatoes and/or mushrooms can be cooked in the grill pan under the rashers of bacon; the fat from the bacon will give them a good flavour.

Cut off the bacon rinds if you wish or just snip the rinds at intervals.

GRILLED
Heat the grill. Put the bacon on the grid in the grill pan and cook, turning occasionally, until it is cooked to your taste.

FRIED
Heat a smear of oil or fat in a frying pan. Add the bacon, and fry over a medium-hot heat, turning occasionally, until the bacon is as you like it.

SAUSAGES
These come in all shapes, sizes and pieces; the thicker the sausage the longer it takes to cook. Have you tried eating sausages with marmalade? I'm told it is delicious, and a boarding school speciality.

Cook as many sausages as you can eat. Always prick the sausages (except for skinless ones) with a fork before cooking to stop the sausages bursting open.

GRILLED
Heat the grill. Put the sausages on the grid in the grill pan, and cook, turning occasionally, until brown and delicious (about 10 to 20 minutes). Thicker sausages may brown on the outside before the middle is cooked, so turn the heat down to medium for the last 5 to 10 minutes of cooking time.

FRIED
Heat a smear of oil or fat in a frying pan, over a medium heat (too hot a pan will make the sausages burst their skins), add the sausages and fry gently, turning occasionally, until they are brown and crispy (10 to 20 minutes). Cook thick sausages

for the longer time, using a lower heat if the outsides start getting too brown.

ROAST

Roast chipolata (thin) sausages are traditionally served as accompaniments to roast turkey and chicken. Roasting is an easy way of cooking sausages if you're not in a hurry. Place the sausages in a lightly-greased tin and bake in a hot oven (400°F/200°C/Gas Mark 6), turning occasionally to cook all over, until crisp and brown (20 to 30 minutes). Thicker sausages take the longer time.

A PROPER BREAKFAST   *Serves 1*
Tastes just as good for lunch or supper.

Preparation and cooking time: 20 minutes.

Use any combination of ingredients according to taste and appetite:
1–4 sausages
1–2 rashers of bacon – streaky, back or collar
1 tomato
3–4 mushrooms
1–2 left-over cold boiled potatoes
1 tbsp oil (for frying)
1–2 eggs
1 slice of bread (for fried bread)
Knob of butter
Several slices of bread (for toast)

The breakfast, apart from the eggs, potatoes and fried bread which are better fried, can be grilled if you prefer. Get everything ready before you actually start cooking: prick the sausages, de-rind the bacon, wash and halve the tomato, wash the mushrooms and slice the potatoes. Warm a plate, put the kettle on ready for tea or coffee, get the bread ready to make the toast, and you're all set to start. In both methods, start cooking the sausages first, as they take the longest to cook, gradually adding the rest of the ingredients to the pan.

FRYING

Heat the oil in a frying pan over a moderate heat and fry the sausages gently, turning occasionally, allowing 10 to 20 minutes for them to cook according to size. When the sausages are half-cooked, put the bacon in the pan with them and fry for 1 to 5 minutes with the sausages, until they are cooked to your taste. Push the sausages and bacon to one side or remove and keep warm. Put the potato slices into the pan and fry until crispy. Fry the tomato and mushrooms at the same time, turning them occasionally until cooked (about 4 to 5 minutes).

Remove the food from the pan and keep hot. Break the eggs into a cup, and slide into the hot fat in the pan over a low heat. Fry them gently until cooked (see page 21). Remove them from the pan and put them with the bacon, sausages, etc. Cut the slice of bread in half, and fry in the fat in the pan, adding a little extra oil or butter if necessary, until golden and crispy, turning to cook both sides (1 to 2 minutes). Remove from the pan and put onto the plate with the rest of the breakfast. Make the toast, coffee or tea, and eat at once.

GRILLING

Heat the grill. Put the tomato halves and mushrooms in the base of the grill pan, arrange the sausages above on the grid, and grill until half cooked (5 to 10 minutes) turning to cook on all sides. Arrange the bacon on the grid with the sausages, and continue cooking for a further 3 to 5 minutes, turning to cook both sides. Remove everything from the pan and keep it warm. Pour the fat from the grill pan into a frying pan, add extra oil or butter if necessary, then fry the potato slices, eggs and fried bread as described above, and enjoy it all with lots of toast, marmalade, and lovely strong coffee or tea.

BANGERS AND MASH

Serves 1

Fast, filling, cheap and tasty!

Preparation and cooking time: 30 minutes.

2–3 potatoes – according to size and appetite (or instant mashed potato – use amount specified in the instructions on the packet)
2–4 sausages – according to size and appetite
Knob of butter

Gravy:
1 tsp flour or cornflour and 1 tsp gravy flavouring powder or 2 tsp gravy granules
1 cup (¼ pt/150ml) water (use the water the potatoes cooked in)
Little fat from the sausages

Peel the potatoes, cut into small, evenly-sized pieces, and cook in boiling, salted water for 10 to 20 minutes, according to size, until soft. Prick the sausages, cook under a hot grill for 10 to 15 minutes, turning frequently, or fry over a medium heat, with a smear of oil to stop them sticking, turning often, for 10 to 15 minutes, until brown. (Make the instant mash, if used, according to the instructions on the packet. Keep it warm.) Test the potatoes for softness, and drain them as soon as they are cooked. Mash them with a fork or potato masher, and beat in the knob of butter. Keep them warm.

Make the gravy, by mixing the flour or cornflour and gravy flavouring powder, or gravy granules, into a smooth paste with a little cold water, or wine, sherry, beer, etc. Add one cup of the vegetable water and any juices from the sausages. Pour the mixture into a small saucepan, and bring to the boil, stirring all the time. Cook until the mixture thickens. Add more liquid if it's too thick. Arrange the mashed potato on a hot plate, stick the sausages round it and pour the gravy over the top.

BRAISED SAUSAGES   *Serves 1*

These take longer to cook, but make a change from the usual fried or grilled sausages. Serve with mashed potatoes.

Preparation and cooking time: 50–60 minutes.

2–3 thick sausages (the spicy, herb sort are the best)
1–2 rashers of streaky bacon
1 small onion (or 2–3 shallots)
2–3 mushrooms
2 tsp oil
1 tsp flour
1 small cup (¼ pt/150ml approx.) wine, beer, or cider or ½
    stock cube dissolved in 1 cup boiling water
Pinch of dried herbs
Pinch of garlic powder
Salt and pepper

Prick the sausages. De-rind and chop the bacon. Peel and thickly slice the onion or peel the shallots and leave whole. Wash the mushrooms and slice if large.

Heat the oil in a casserole or thick saucepan, over a moderate heat, and lightly brown the sausages. Remove them from the pan.

Add the bacon and onion, and fry for 2 to 3 minutes. Stir in the flour, and gradually add the wine, beer, cider or stock, stirring as the sauce thickens.

Return the sausages to the pan. Add the mushrooms, herbs, garlic, salt and pepper. Reheat, then put on the lid, lower the heat and leave to simmer gently for 35 to 45 minutes, removing the lid for the last 15 minutes of cooking time. Add a little more liquid if it gets too dry.

SAVOURY SAUSAGE-MEAT PIE

Serves 1

The apple gives the sausage-meat a tangy taste.

Preparation and cooking time: 50 minutes.

3–4 potato pieces (or a large serving of instant mashed potato, use amount specified in the instructions on the packet)
1 cooking apple
1 onion
2 tomatoes (tinned or fresh)
1 tsp sugar
4 oz (100g) sausage-meat (or 2–4 sausages)
Knob of butter

Prepare the mashed potato (see page 107) or make up the instant potato as instructed on the packet. Peel, core and slice the apple. Peel and chop the onion. Slice the fresh tomatoes, or drain and slice the tinned tomatoes.

Place the apple slices in the base of a greased, oven-proof dish. Sprinkle with the sugar. If using sausages, slit the sausage skins to remove the sausage-meat and dispose of the skins. Mix the chopped onion with the sausage-meat or the skinned sausages and spread the sausage mixture over the apples.

Spoon the mashed potato round the dish to make a border or 'nest' for the sausage. Cover the sausage with the tomatoes. Dot the potato with the butter, and bake in an oven (400°F/200°C/Gas Mark 6) for 30 minutes, until the sausage is cooked and the potato is crisp and golden-brown on top.

TOAD IN THE HOLE
Serves 1

You can use either large sausages (toads) or chipolatas (frogs) for this meal, whichever you prefer! Some people believe that a better Yorkshire Pudding is made if the ingredients are mixed together first and the batter is then left to stand in the fridge while you prepare the rest of the meal. Alternatively, make the batter while the sausages are cooking.

Preparation and cooking time: 45–55 minutes.

3–6 sausages (according to appetite and size)
1 tbsp cooking oil

Yorkshire Pudding batter:
2 heaped tbsp plain flour
Pinch of salt
1 egg
1 cup (¼ pt/150ml) milk

Heat the oven (425°F/220°C/Gas Mark 7–8). Prick the sausages. Put them into a baking tin with the oil. (Any baking tin can be used, but not one with a loose base. You do not get as good a result with a pyrex-type dish.) Cook the chipolatas for 5 minutes or the larger ones for 10 minutes.

Make the batter while the sausages are cooking. Put the flour and salt in a basin, add the egg, and beat it into the flour, gradually adding the milk, to make a smooth batter. (This is easier with a hand or electric mixer, but with a bit of old-fashioned effort you can get just as good a result using a whisk, wooden spoon or even a fork.) Pour the batter into the baking tin on top of the hot sausages. Bake for a further 20 to 25 minutes, until the Yorkshire pud is golden. Try not to open the oven door for the first 10 to 15 minutes, so that the pudding will rise well. Serve at once.

HAWAIIAN SAUSAGES

Serves 1

An unusual variation on the sausage and bean theme.

Preparation and cooking time: 30 minutes.

3–6 sausages, according to size and appetite
½ small can (7¾ oz/220g size) pineapple rings
1 small onion (or 2 spring onions)
Knob of butter
1 small can (7.9 oz/225g) baked beans
1 tsp vinegar
Salt and pepper

Prick the sausages. Fry or grill them until cooked and brown (see page 133). Add 1 or 2 pineapple rings and heat through with the sausages for a minute or two. Save 2 sausages, and keep hot with the pineapple rings (for decoration). Slice the rest of the sausages.

Peel and slice the onion, or wash and chop the spring onions. Chop another 1 or 2 pineapple rings.

Heat the butter in a saucepan over a moderate heat, and fry the onion and pineapple pieces until soft (2 to 3 minutes). Add the beans, sliced sausages, vinegar, salt and pepper, and simmer for 3 to 4 minutes.

Pour into a warm serving dish. Decorate with the whole sausages and pineapple rings you are keeping hot. Serve with crispy bread rolls or hot toast.

SAUSAGE AND BACON HUBBLE BUBBLE *Serves 1*

A tasty way of using up odds and ends from the fridge.

Preparation and cooking time: 30 minutes.

2–3 cooked boiled potatoes
1 small onion
1 rasher of bacon
2–4 sausages
2 tsp oil (for frying)
1 egg
½ cup milk
Salt and pepper

Heat the oven (375°F/190°C/Gas Mark 5–6). Grease an oven-proof dish.

Slice the cooked potatoes. Peel and chop the onion. De-rind the bacon. Prick the sausages.

Heat the oil in a frying pan, and fry the sausages, bacon and onion gently for 5 minutes, turning frequently.

Place the potato slices in the dish. Arrange the onions, sausages and bacon on top. Beat the egg with the milk, salt and pepper in a small basin, using a whisk or fork. Pour the egg mixture over the top, and bake in a hot oven for about 15 minutes, until the egg mixture is set.

CHEESY SAUSAGES

Serves 1

A quick and tasty lunch or supper.

Preparation and cooking time: 25 minutes.

2 or 3 thick sausages
2 or 3 rashers of back bacon
1–2 oz (25–50g) Cheddar cheese
1 tbsp pickle (or sweet chutney)
Few wooden cocktail sticks or toothpicks
1–2 slices of bread
Little butter

Prick the sausages with a fork. Grill them under a moderate heat for about 15 minutes. Make a slit in each sausage, lengthways, and wedge a slice of cheese in each slit. Cut the rind from the bacon, and spread with the chutney.

7. Cheesy sausages

Wrap the bacon round the sausages and pin securely with cocktail sticks or toothpicks (not plastic ones!). Return to the hot grill, and cook for about 5 minutes, until the bacon is crisp and the cheese is melting. Toast the bread, spread with the butter and serve with the sausages.

GAMMON STEAK WITH PINEAPPLE OR FRIED EGG

Serves 1

Buy a thick slice (½ in/1.25cm at least) of gammon, if possible, as thin slices just go crispy, like bacon. Serve with boiled new potatoes and salad in summer and sauté or jacket potatoes and peas in winter.

Preparation and cooking time: 6–10 minutes according to taste.

1 steak or slice (about 6 oz/175g) gammon
Little oil
1–2 tinned pineapple rings
   or 1 egg

GRILLED

Heat the grill. Snip the gammon rind at intervals. Brush or wipe both sides of the gammon with a smear of oil. Place the gammon on the grid of the grill pan and cook each side under the hot grill for 3 to 5 minutes, until brown. Put the pineapple slices on top of the gammon and heat for a few moments or fry the egg in a frying pan, in a little hot fat. Serve the gammon with the pineapple slices or with the egg on top.

FRIED

Snip the gammon rind at intervals. Heat a smear of oil or fat in a frying pan. Add the gammon and cook each side for 3 to 5 minutes, until brown. Add the pineapple rings to the pan and heat for a few moments or fry the egg in the hot fat. Serve the gammon with the pineapple rings or with the egg on top.

ST DAVID'S DAY SUPPER

Serves 2

Leeks, of course, are the main ingredients.

Preparation and cooking time: 40 minutes.

5–6 potatoes
2 medium-sized leeks
Salt and pepper
4 oz (100g) cooked ham
1 small can (10.4 oz/295g) cream of chicken soup
1 tomato

Wash and peel the potatoes. Cut them into thick slices. Cut off the roots and leaves of the leeks and wash thoroughly (see page 98) and slice.

Put the potato and leek slices in a saucepan, cover with boiling, salted water, and cook for 8 to 10 minutes, until half cooked. Drain well.

Grease an oven-proof dish, put the vegetable mixture into the dish, and sprinkle with the salt and pepper. Chop the ham. Put the ham on top of the vegetables. Pour the chicken soup over the top, and heat through in the oven (400°F/200°C/Gas Mark 6) for about 20 minutes.

Wash and slice the tomato and place on top of the vegetables for the last 5 minutes of cooking time. Serve with hot bread rolls and butter.

LUNCHEON MEAT PATTIES   *Serves 1*

Cheap and tasty, and filling enough for lunch or supper if
served with fried eggs.

Preparation and cooking time: 20 minutes.

3–4 potatoes
1 small onion
4 oz (100g) luncheon meat (canned or sliced)
A little beaten egg
Salt and pepper
Pinch of dried herbs
Oil (for frying)
Knob of butter (for frying)

Peel and thickly slice the potatoes. Cook them in boiling,
salted water for 10 minutes, until soft. Drain them and mash
well.

Peel and finely chop or grate the onion. Chop the
luncheon meat.

Mix together the potato, onion, luncheon meat, and bind
with the well-beaten egg, adding sufficient egg to hold it all
together. Season with the salt, pepper and herbs. Form the
mixture into 3 or 4 equal portions. Shape each into a ball and
then flatten to form 'beefburger' shapes about ¾ in (2cm)
thick.

Heat the oil and butter in a frying pan, and fry over a
moderate heat for 3 to 5 minutes, turning to cook both sides,
until crisp and golden brown. Serve with fresh or fried
tomatoes and/or a couple of fried eggs, if you're really
hungry.

BACON-STUFFED COURGETTES
Serves 1

In the autumn, when marrows are cheap, you can make a very economical and tasty meal using marrow instead.

Preparation and cooking time: 1 hour.

1 onion
4 oz (100g/2–3 rashers) bacon – odd slices of bacon, sometimes sold cheaply as they are left-over end pieces, are suitable for this dish too
1 tomato
2 tsp cooking oil
½ tsp dried mixed herbs
Salt and pepper
2 medium courgettes

Peel and chop the onion. Cut the rind from the bacon; cut or chop it into small pieces. Chop the tomato. Heat the oil in a frying pan, add the onion and fry gently for 3 to 4 minutes, until soft. Add the bacon, and cook for a further 8 to 10 minutes, stirring well. Add the tomato and seasoning.

Wash the courgettes in cold water and cut a wedge-shaped 'lid' along the length of each courgette, to leave a hollow. Pile the filling into the hollow. Put the courgettes carefully into a greased, oven-proof dish and top with the 'lids'. Cover with a piece of foil and bake in a moderate oven (350°F/180°C/Gas Mark 4–5) for about 45 minutes. Serve with hot, brown bread rolls and butter, and a green salad.

VEGETABLE MARROW
These are often fairly large, so increase the quantity of stuffing, and make enough for several people. Remove a thick slice from the top of the marrow (to be used later). Scoop out the seeds. Fill the marrow with the prepared stuffing. Top with the 'lid' you sliced off. Brush lightly with a little cooking oil or softened butter, and carefully put the marrow on a greased baking dish. Bake in a moderate oven (350°F/180°C/Gas Mark 4–5) for about 1 hour.

FARMHOUSE SUPPER

Serves 1

A tasty way of using up cooked potato and food from the fridge to make a meal.

Preparation and cooking time: 20 minutes.

3–4 cooked, boiled potatoes (see page 107 if you don't have any cooked)
1 small onion
1–2 rashers of bacon
½ small green pepper
1 oz (25g) cheese
Little oil for frying
Knob of butter
1–2 eggs

Slice and dice the potatoes. Peel and chop the onion. De-rind and dice the bacon. Core and chop the pepper. Grate the cheese.

Heat the oil in a frying pan, add the bacon, and fry gently for 3 to 4 minutes. Remove the bacon from the pan and save on a saucer.

Put the potatoes, onion and green pepper into the hot fat in the pan, and continue to fry gently for 5 to 10 minutes, until lightly browned.

Mix the bacon with the vegetables and place in an oven-proof dish. Melt the butter in the pan and fry the eggs. Carefully put the eggs on top of the vegetables and bacon. Cover with the grated cheese, and brown for a few minutes under a hot grill, until the cheese is bubbly. Serve at once.

7

Offal and Cooked Meats

This means kidney, liver, tripe and sweetbreads etc. They are extraordinarily cheap, and besides being such good value for money, are very nourishing. Lamb's liver and kidney are more expensive than pig's liver and kidney which have a stronger taste, are very cheap, and make a tasty meal as well.

FRIED LIVER AND BACON WITH FRIED ONIONS
Serves 1

Lamb's liver is delicious fried, but if you are really counting the pennies, buy pig's liver and soak it for an hour in a little milk to give it a more delicate flavour.

Preparation and cooking time: 15 minutes (plus 30–60 minutes soaking time for the pig's liver).

4–6 oz (100–175g) lamb's or pig's liver (sliced)
Milk (for soaking)
1 rasher of bacon
1 onion
Little oil (for frying)
Knob of butter (for frying)

Gravy:
2 tsp gravy granules
  or 1 tsp flour (or cornflour) and 1 tsp gravy flavouring powder
1 tsp cold water, sherry or wine (optional)
½ cup water (or water used in cooking the vegetables)

Put the pig's liver slices in a shallow dish, cover with a little milk, and leave to soak for 30 to 60 minutes. Lamb's liver does not need soaking. De-rind the bacon. Peel and slice the onion into rings. Dry the liver on kitchen paper. Heat the oil and butter in a frying pan over a moderate heat. Add the onion slices and fry for 3 to 4 minutes, stirring frequently, until soft. Push the onion to one side of the pan and stir occasionally while frying the bacon and liver.

Put the bacon and liver in the hot fat in the pan, and fry gently for 3 to 5 minutes, turning frequently, until cooked to taste – liver should be soft on the outside, not crispy. Remove the liver, bacon and onion from the pan and serve on a hot plate.

Either pour the meat juices from the pan over the liver and serve with crusty new bread; or make gravy with the juices and serve with boiled potatoes and a green vegetable. For the gravy: mix the gravy granules (or flour and gravy flavouring powder) into a smooth paste with the sherry, wine or cold water. Add the half cup of vegetable water or cold water and mix well. Pour onto the meat juices in the pan, stirring well. Bring to the boil, stirring all the time until the gravy thickens. Pour over the liver and vegetables.

SAVOURY CORNED BEEF HASH

Serves 1

Every cowboy's favourite standby!

Preparation and cooking time: 30 minutes.

3–4 potatoes
½ small onion
2–4 oz (50–100g) corned beef
Salt and pepper
1 tbsp oil (for frying)
1 egg
1 tsp tomato purée (or ketchup)
1 tbsp hot water
A dash of Worcester sauce
A dash of tabasco sauce

Peel the potatoes, cut into large dice, and cook for 5 to 6 minutes, in boiling, salted water, until half cooked. Drain well.

Peel and finely chop the onion. Dice the corned beef. Mix together the potato cubes, onion and corned beef. Season with salt and pepper. Grease well a frying pan with oil and put the meat and potato mixture into the pan.

Beat the egg. Dissolve the tomato purée or ketchup in 1 tbsp of hot water, beat this into the egg, add the Worcester and tabasco sauces then pour onto the meat mixture. Fry gently for about 15 minutes, stirring occasionally. Serve hot.

I have known people to make this gourmet dish using cooked rice instead of cooked potatoes, but it has not been particularly successful.

SAUCY LIVER SAVOURY
Serves 1

This is a real money saver, as it can be made with the cheaper pig's liver (but remember to allow the soaking time to give the liver a more delicate flavour – see method below). Serve with creamy, mashed potatoes or plain boiled rice or crusty bread rolls and butter, and a green salad.

Preparation and cooking time: 25 minutes (plus 30–60 minutes soaking time).

4–6 oz (100–175g) pig's or lamb's liver
½ cup cold milk
1 onion
Clove of garlic (or pinch of garlic powder or garlic paste)
Knob of butter (for frying)
Little oil (for frying)
1 tsp flour
1 tbsp tomato purée (or tomato ketchup)
Pinch of dried mixed herbs
Salt and pepper
½ stock cube and ½ cup hot water

Cut the liver into 1 in (2.5cm) strips, and soak the pig's liver in cold milk for 30 to 60 minutes, if possible. Lamb's liver need not be soaked. Peel and slice the onion. Peel and chop the fresh garlic. Remove the liver from the milk, but reserve the milk to use in the sauce.

Heat the butter and oil in a frying pan over a moderate heat, and fry the onion for 2 to 3 minutes, stirring occasionally, until just soft. Add the liver pieces, fry gently, turning frequently to brown on all sides (3 to 5 minutes). Stir in the flour, garlic, tomato purée, herbs, salt and pepper. Remove from the heat. Dissolve the stock cube in the hot water. Gradually mix in the stock and milk, return to the heat and stir continuously until the sauce thickens. Lower the heat, cover the pan and leave to simmer for 10 minutes until the liver is tender.

LIVER HOT POT

Serves 1

Make this with the really cheap pig's liver if you're counting the pennies, but remember to soak the slices to give it a more delicate flavour. Serve hot with a green vegetable.

Preparation and cooking time: 1 hour (plus 30–60 minutes soaking time).

4–6 oz (100–175g) lamb's or pig's liver (sliced)
Milk (for soaking)
3–4 potatoes
1 onion
1 tomato
2–3 mushrooms
Oil (for frying)
Salt and pepper
Pinch of dried herbs
½ stock cube
½ cup hot water
Knob of butter

Soak the pig's liver slices in milk for 30 to 60 minutes, if possible. Lamb's liver need not be soaked. Peel the potatoes, thickly slice them (¼ in/0.5cm) and cook for 5 minutes in boiling, salted water, until partly cooked. Drain them. Peel and slice the onion into rings. Wash and slice the tomato and mushrooms. Heat the oil in a frying pan, and fry the onion rings gently for 2 to 3 minutes, until just soft. Push them to one side of the pan. Add the liver slices and fry these, turning to cook both sides, for 1 to 2 minutes.

Grease an oven-proof dish or casserole, and arrange the slices of onion, liver, mushrooms and tomato in layers. Sprinkle with the salt, pepper and herbs. Dissolve the stock cube in the ½ cup of hot water and pour the stock into the casserole. Cover the casserole with a thick layer of the sliced potatoes. Dot the potatoes with the butter, and bake in an oven (375°F/190°C/Gas Mark 5–6) for about 35 to 45 minutes, until the potatoes are brown and crispy on the top.

KIDNEY STROGANOFF

Serves 1

A special kidney dish, but much cheaper than beef stroganoff, so treat yourself to lamb's kidneys and enjoy them. Serve with plain, boiled rice.

Preparation and cooking time: 35 minutes.

1 small onion
2–3 mushrooms
3–4 lamb's kidneys
Knob of butter (for frying)
1 tsp oil (for frying)
1 tsp flour (or cornflour)
Salt and pepper
⅔ cup milk (just under ¼ pint/150ml)
½ cup (3 oz/75g) raw, long grain rice
2 tbsp plain yoghurt

Peel and chop the onion. Wash and slice the mushrooms. Cut the kidneys in half lengthways. Remove the white fatty core and cut the kidneys into quarters

Melt the butter and oil in a saucepan over a moderate heat, and fry the onion gently for 2 to 3 minutes to soften. Add the mushrooms and stir. Add the kidneys, flour, salt and pepper, and continue to cook for another 3 to 5 minutes until the kidneys are browned on all sides.

Remove the pan from the heat and gradually stir in the milk. Return to the heat and slowly bring the sauce to the boil, stirring gently all the time as the sauce thickens. Lower the heat, cover the pan and simmer very gently for 10 to 15 minutes, until the kidneys are cooked. Cook the rice (while the kidneys are simmering) in boiling, salted water. Stir the yoghurt into the kidney sauce. Drain the rice and serve hot with the kidneys.

QUICK KIDNEY SPECIAL   *Serves 1*

This is delicious made with lamb's kidney, and makes a complete supper with sauté potatoes, served with a green salad.

Preparation and cooking time: 35 minutes.

3–4 small potatoes
1 small onion
2–3 lamb's kidneys
Oil (for frying)
Knob of butter (for frying)
Salt and pepper
Pinch of garlic powder (or clove of garlic)
1 tbsp sherry (or wine)
1 tbsp cream (or sour cream or plain yoghurt)

Peel the potatoes. Slice them thickly (¼ in/0.5cm) and cook gently in boiling, salted water for 5 to 10 minutes, until just soft. Drain them.

Peel the onion, slice it into thin rings. Cut the kidneys in halves, and remove the fatty white core. Then cut the kidneys into quarters.

Heat the oil and butter in a frying pan, and fry the potatoes, turning occasionally, for a few minutes, until golden and crispy. Remove from the pan, drain on kitchen paper and keep warm on a hot plate.

Add a little more butter to the frying pan if necessary, and fry the onion rings and kidneys over a gentle heat, stirring gently, for 5 to 10 minutes, until the kidneys are cooked. Season with the salt and pepper and garlic. Stir in the sherry and cream, stirring to heat thoroughly, but do not allow to boil. Make the potatoes into a 'nest'. Pour the kidneys and sauce into the middle of the potatoes and serve at once.

KIDNEY DINNER

Serves 1

This can be made with lamb's kidneys or the cheaper pig's kidney, according to how rich you are feeling – both are tasty and delicious. Serve with boiled rice or boiled new potatoes; these can be prepared in advance and kept warm while the kidneys are cooking.

Preparation and cooking time: 20 minutes.

8 oz (225g/3–4) lamb's kidneys or (1–1½) pig's kidneys
1 tsp oil (for frying)
Knob of butter (for frying)
½ small tin (10.4 oz/295g size) of kidney (or oxtail) soup
1 tsp flour (or cornflour) and ½ tsp gravy flavouring powder
  or 2 tsp gravy granules
1 tbsp water or sherry or wine (your choice)
1 tbsp cream (optional)

Cut the kidneys in half, lengthways, and remove the white, fatty core. Cut the kidneys into pieces.

Heat the oil and butter gently in a saucepan. Add the kidneys and fry over a moderate heat, stirring until the kidneys are browned on all sides. Gradually stir in about 1 cup of soup and leave to simmer for 10 minutes, over a very low heat, until the kidneys are tender.

Mix the flour and gravy flavouring powder (or gravy granules) into a smooth paste with the sherry, wine or water, and add to the kidney sauce, stirring as the sauce thickens. Stir in the cream, if using, and heat through, but do not let the cream boil.

155

KEBABS   *Serves 1*

This is an economical recipe, using kidney, sausages and bacon, instead of the much more expensive steak, cubed pork or lamb. The supermarkets sell packets of ready-prepared assorted kebab meats, which are good value, as it is rather expensive buying small quantities of different meats. Serve with boiled rice or bread rolls, and a green salad and barbecue sauce.

Preparation and cooking time: 20–25 minutes.

Use any mixture of the following:

1–2 rashers of bacon
1–2 chipolata sausages
1–2 lamb's kidneys
2–4 button mushrooms
1–2 tomatoes
Few pieces of green pepper
1 onion
1–2 pickled onions
Few pineapple cubes
Allow 1–2 long skewers per person
Oil for cooking

Heat the oven (400°F/200°C/Gas Mark 6–7) or the grill. Start cooking the rice, if used, in boiling salted water (see page 118). Prepare the salad and put aside.

Assemble and prepare your chosen ingredients as follows. De-rind the bacon. Cut the rashers in half to make them shorter in length, and roll them into little bacon rolls. Twist and halve the chipolata sausages. Halve the kidneys lengthways and remove the white, fatty core. Wash the mushrooms. Wash the tomatoes, cut into halves or quarters, according to size. Slice the green pepper into chunks. Peel the onion and cut into quarters. Drain the pickled onions and the pineapple cubes.

8. Kebabs

Thread the skewers with the chosen food, arranging it as you wish. Brush or wipe with oil. Either grill under a moderate grill on the grill rack, or balance the skewers across a baking tin in the hot oven, and cook for about 15 minutes, turning frequently. Drain the rice. Serve the kebabs on the skewers – be careful: they will be hot, so have a paper napkin handy.

8
Fish

Fresh or frozen fish can be used in these recipes according to availability. Fishmongers and market stalls sell wet fish, but most fish sold in the supermarkets is frozen and ready to use. The inevitable fish finger is well-known and widely available, along with other packets of frozen fish ready for frying. These need not be deep-fried, but are good cooked in a frying pan in a little butter and oil, or grilled. Eaten with bread, butter and tomato sauce these make a really quick supper. There are also many commercially-frozen fish dishes sold in the supermarkets, which are quite cheap, and quick and easy to cook, often by simply heating the packets in a saucepan of boiling water. Follow the instructions given on the packet carefully (short cuts aren't usually very successful) and serve with boiled or mashed potatoes, fresh or frozen vegetables, bread rolls or a side salad.

FRIED FISH WITH BUTTER

Serves 1

Serve with plain boiled potatoes.

Preparation and cooking time: 15–20 minutes (according to the type of fish used).

2–4 potato pieces
6–8 oz (175–225g) fillet of white fish (fresh or frozen) – cod, haddock, or plaice are the cheapest
1–2 oz (25–50g) butter
1 tsp cooking oil
Parsley (optional)
Slice of lemon (optional)

Peel and boil the potatoes (see page 107). Wash and dry the fish on kitchen paper.

Melt the butter in a frying pan with the oil (the oil stops the butter going too brown), add the fish and fry until tender (about 5 to 10 minutes), spooning the melted butter over it as it cooks. (The thicker the fish the longer it will take to cook.)

Lift the fish carefully onto a warm plate, add a little chopped parsley (if used) to the butter in the pan and heat thoroughly. Pour the buttery juice over the fish and garnish with the lemon slice. Drain the potatoes and serve.

FRIED OR GRILLED TROUT (OR MACKEREL)

Serves 1

These can be bought quite cheaply fresh from trout farms, but frozen trout are also good value, as they provide a filling meal with just bread and butter. Mackerel are cheap, delicious and are cooked in the same way.

Preparation and cooking time: 15–20 minutes.

1 trout or mackerel
1 tsp oil (for frying)
½ oz (12g) butter
Slice of lemon (optional)
Vinegar (optional)

Clean the fish by removing its head, entrails, fins and gills. (The fishmonger will usually do this for you. Frozen fish is already cleaned.)

FRIED
Heat the oil and butter in a frying pan, and fry the fish over a moderate heat, for about 5 minutes on each side.

GRILLED
Dot with the butter and grill on both sides until done (about 5 minutes each side for a medium-sized fish).

Serve with a slice of lemon, or vinegar, and brown or French bread and butter.

CHEESY COD STEAKS *Serves 1*

Thick pieces of cod or haddock, or frozen fish steaks can be used. The frozen steaks are easy to cook and keep a good shape as they are individually wrapped and so can be separated easily while still frozen.

Preparation and cooking time: 20 minutes.

6–8 oz (175–225g) piece of cod (or 1–2 frozen fish steaks)
Salt and pepper
½ slice of bread
½ oz (12g) Cheddar cheese
½ oz (12g) butter

Wipe the fish and season with salt and pepper. Grate or crumble the bread, grate or finely chop the cheese, and mix together.

Put the fish in the base of a greased grill pan, dot with half the butter and grill for 5 minutes. Turn the fish over, cover with the cheese mixture, dot with the remaining butter and grill for another 5 minutes.

Serve on a warm plate.

TOMATO FISH BAKE

Serves 1

Brill is very tasty in this recipe, but cod or haddock are good too (and probably cheaper).

Preparation and cooking time: 35 minutes.

1 portion (6 oz/150g) fillet of brill, cod or haddock
2 tsp cooking oil
½ small onion
½ small can (8 oz/230g size) tomatoes (or use 1 or 2 fresh tomatoes)
Salt and pepper
¼ green pepper (optional)
1 stick of celery (optional)

Put the fish in a greased oven-proof dish.

Heat the oil in a small saucepan, chop the onion and fry it gently in the oil, until soft (2 to 3 minutes).

Add the tinned tomatoes or chopped fresh tomatoes and seasoning. Bring to the boil and cook gently until the liquid is reduced to a thin purée (3 to 5 minutes).

Chop the celery and/or pepper if used, stir into the tomato mixture, and spoon the sauce over the fish. Cover with a lid or cooking foil, and bake for about 20 minutes in an oven (375°F/190°C/Gas Mark 5). Serve hot.

TUNA BAKE

Serve with crispy bread rolls or toast.

Preparation and cooking time: 20 minutes.

½–1 can (200g size) tuna fish (use the rest for sandwiches
   or in Tuna Fiesta or Tuna Continental)
½ can (10 oz/298g size) condensed mushroom soup
1 slice of bread (crumbled into breadcrumbs)
1 oz (25g) butter
Few mushrooms (optional)

Drain the tuna fish and flake it into large flakes. Heat the
soup in a saucepan, add the fish and cook for 2 to 3 minutes.

Pour the mixture into a heat-proof dish. Sprinkle with the
breadcrumbs and dot with half the butter. Grill for 5 minutes
or until golden brown.

Meanwhile wash the mushrooms, if used, melt the
remaining butter in the pan, add the mushrooms and cook
gently for 4 to 5 minutes. Place on top of the hot tuna bake
and serve at once.

Do not leave the remainder of the tuna fish or the soup in
the cans. Put them into covered containers or cups in the
fridge and use within 24 hours.

TUNA FIESTA

Serve with boiled rice or mashed potatoes.

Preparation and cooking time: 25 minutes.

½ cup (3 oz/75g) long grained rice, or 2–4 potato pieces
1 small onion
½ oz (12g) margarine (or butter or 1 tsp cooking oil)
2 oz (50g) mushrooms
½ green pepper
2 oz (50g) peas
2 tbsp tinned tomato soup
Salt and pepper
Garlic powder
½ can (200g size) tuna fish (use the rest for sandwiches or in Tuna Bake or Tuna Continental)

Peel the potatoes (or wash the rice) and boil (see pages 107 and 118).

Peel and slice the onion and fry it gently in the butter or oil in a saucepan, until soft (2 to 3 minutes).

Wash and slice the mushrooms and pepper. Add them to the onion and fry gently, until soft (2 minutes). Add the peas, tomato soup, salt, pepper and garlic. Gently stir in the drained tuna and cook for a few minutes, until hot.

Strain the potatoes and mash (or drain and fork the rice). Spoon the potatoes or rice onto a plate, press into a ring and pour the tuna sauce into the middle.

Do not leave the remainder of the tuna fish or soup in the cans. Put them into covered containers or cups in the fridge and use within 24 hours.

TUNA CONTINENTAL

Serves 2–4

This stretches left-over tuna into a lunch for several people, according to the amount of tuna available and your appetites.

Preparation and cooking time: 20 minutes.

2 oz (50g) rice per person
1 onion
1 clove of garlic or ¼ tsp ground garlic
½–1 green pepper
2–3 sticks of celery
4 oz (100g) mushrooms
1 tbsp oil (for frying)
1 × 290g can tomato, mushroom or celery soup
4 oz (100g) frozen peas or mixed vegetables
Salt and black pepper
½ can (200g size) tuna fish
Lemon wedges and parsley (for garnish)

Put the rice on to cook in a pan of boiling salted water, allowing 10 to 15 minutes for white rice, 20 to 25 minutes for brown rice, or as directed on the packet.

Peel and chop the onion. Peel and crush the fresh garlic. Wash and chop the pepper and celery. Slice the mushrooms.

Heat the oil in a pan over a moderate heat and fry the onion with the garlic for 2 to 3 minutes, until beginning to soften. Add the pepper and celery and fry for a further 4 to 5 minutes, then stir in the sliced mushrooms and cook for another minute or two until just soft. Stir in the chosen soup, stir in the peas or mixed vegetables (these can be cooked from frozen), and cook for a further 3 to 5 minutes until the sauce is hot, thick and tasty. Season to taste and stir in the tuna, being careful not to break it up too small. Heat thoroughly over a low heat, stirring very gently.

Drain the rice and arrange in a ring on a serving dish. Pour the tuna sauce into the ring and serve hot, garnished with a little fresh snipped parsley and lemon wedges.

COD IN CIDER

Serves 1

White wine can be used instead of cider for a taste of real luxury!

Preparation and cooking time: 30–35 minutes.

1 small onion
Slice of lemon (optional)
Salt and pepper
6–8 oz (175–225g) piece of cod (or 1–2 frozen fish steaks)
½ cup cider
½ slice of bread
½ oz (12g) butter

Grease an oven-proof dish.

Peel and slice the onion finely, and arrange half in the dish. Add a squeeze of lemon, salt and pepper. Put the fish on top, cover with the rest of the onion and another squeeze of lemon. Carefully pour in the cider.

Crumble the bread into crumbs and sprinkle on top of the fish. Dot with the butter.

Bake in a moderate oven (375°F/190°C/Gas Mark 5) until golden brown.

QUICK KIPPER PÂTÉ

Serves 1 or 2

This isn't really a pâté recipe, more a kind of posh spread. It's a delicious way to use up a half packet of defrosted kipper fillets. For a change of flavour, mix the mashed fish with cream cheese instead of, or mixed with, the softened butter.

Preparation time: 10 minutes plus chilling time if possible.

½–1 170g size packet of cooked kipper fillets
1–2 oz (25–50g) butter (nicer than margarine!)
1–2 tsp lemon juice
Salt and black pepper
Pinch of cayenne pepper and/or pinch of nutmeg (optional)
Handful of fresh chives or 2 or 3 spring onions (optional)

Cook the fish (if not already cooked) according to the instructions on the packet. Remove and discard any skin or stray bones from the fish. Put the fish into a basin, and mash it well with a fork.

Soften the butter (but don't melt it), and beat enough butter into the fish to make a soft pâté. Season well with lemon juice, salt, pepper and spices, and stir in a few washed, finely snipped chives or chopped spring onions if liked.

Spoon into 1 or 2 little ramekin dishes, cover with cling film and chill in the fridge until needed.

Serve with fresh brown bread and butter, granary rolls or French bread.

9
Beef

Generally the most expensive meat, especially if you buy the cuts for grilling or roasting. However, stewing steak and mince are much cheaper and can be made into delicious dishes, but they do take longer to prepare and cook, as the cheaper the meat the longer the cooking time.

BEEF CASSEROLE OR STEW   *Serves 1*
You can use any mixture of stewing beef and vegetables to make a casserole (cooked in the oven) or a stew (simmered in a covered pan on top of the stove), so just combine the vegetables you like. If you want the meal to go further add

extra vegetables. Some supermarkets sell small packets of mixed root vegetables especially for casseroles. These are useful as you only need a small amount of each vegetable. As this dish is easier to cook in larger quantities (smaller quantities tend to dry up during cooking) why not double or triple the ingredients to make enough for 2 or 3 friends?

Preparation and cooking time: 1 hour 50 minutes – 2 hours 50 minutes.

(For one person cook 4 oz stewing steak for 1 hour 30 minutes; for 2 people cook 8 oz stewing steak for about 2 hours; for larger quantities cook for 2 hours 30 minutes.)

1 onion
Little oil or fat (for frying)
4–6 oz (100–175g) stewing steak
1 oz (25g) kidney (optional) – ox kidney is usually stewed
1 stock cube
½ glass of wine or beer (optional)

Vegetables – any mixture according to taste:
1 carrot – peeled and sliced
Piece of swede (or small turnip) – peeled thickly, cut into 1 in (2.5cm) chunks
Stick of celery – washed and cut into ½ in (1.25cm) lengths
½ green pepper – washed, with the core and seeds removed, cut into short strips
1 courgette (or small aubergine) – washed, cut into ½ in (1.25cm) pieces
1 potato – peeled, cut into 1 in (2.5cm) chunks
1 oz (25g) mushrooms – washed, sliced
Clove of garlic – peeled, finely chopped
1 cup of water
Pinch of herbs
Garlic powder
Salt and pepper

(continued overleaf)

(Beef Casserole or Stew continued)

For thicker gravy:

½ tsp gravy flavouring powder and 1 tsp flour (or cornflour) or 2 tsp gravy granules

A little wine, beer or water to mix

Peel and slice the onion and fry it gently in a casserole or a saucepan, until soft (about 2 to 3 minutes).

Cut the meat into 1 in (2.5cm) pieces, (kidney in ½ in (1cm) pieces), add to the onion in the pan, and fry until brown (3 to 5 minutes) stirring so that it cooks evenly. Stir in the stock cube and add the wine or beer if used.

Prepare the vegetables but do no cut them too small. Add them to the meat. Stir in the water so that it just covers the meat and vegetables. Add the herbs, salt, pepper and garlic powder. Bring to the boil and stir well.

Then either put the covered casserole dish in the middle of a moderate oven (325°F/170°C/Gas Mark 3–4), or lower the heat and leave to simmer with the lid on the pan for 1½ hours to 2½ hours according to the amount of meat used, stirring occasionally. If it seems to be drying up, add a little more wine, beer or water.

If you like the gravy thicker, mix the gravy flavouring powder and flour (or cornflour) or gravy granules into a thin paste with a little wine, beer or water, and add to the gravy in the dish for the last half hour of cooking time.

Serve very hot, on its own, or with jacket spuds (cooked in the oven with the casserole), boiled potatoes or hot French bread and butter.

SHEPHERD'S PIE

Serves 1

Forget about school dinners, this can be made into a really delicious meal! For a change, add a little grated cheese to the potato topping, and sprinkle the top with grated cheese before grilling. The meat mixture can also be served on its own, or with boiled or mashed potatoes and vegetables.

Preparation and cooking time: 55 minutes.

1 small onion
2 tsp oil or fat (for frying)
4 oz (100g) minced beef
Little wine or beer (if you have any opened)
2 tsp tomato ketchup (optional)
Shake of Worcester sauce (optional)
½ stock cube
½ cup water
2–3 potatoes
½ oz (12g) butter or margarine
1 tomato (optional)

Peel and chop the onion. Put the oil or fat in a saucepan, and fry the onion gently for 2 to 3 minutes, until soft. Add the minced meat, and continue to fry gently, stirring all the time, until the meat is brown (about 2 to 3 minutes). Add the wine or beer, and sauces, stock cube and water. Stir well. Bring to the boil, then reduce the heat and leave to simmer for 20 to 30 minutes, until the meat is tender.

Meanwhile, peel the potatoes, cut them into evenly-sized pieces, and cook in boiling, salted water for 15 to 20 minutes, until soft. Drain and mash them with a potato masher or fork. Add the butter and beat until creamy. Pour the meat mixture into an oven-proof dish, cover with the mashed potato and fork down smoothly. Dot the top with a little butter, top with a sliced tomato if liked, and grill under a hot grill for a minute or two, until golden brown, or put on the top shelf of a hot oven (400°F/200°C/Gas Mark 6) for 5 to 10 minutes, until it is brown on top.

171

INSTANT SHEPHERD'S PIE

This really is an 'instant' meal, but is made quite tasty by adding a dash of your favourite sauces to the meat.

Preparation and cooking time: 10 minutes.

1 small tin (7 oz/198g) minced steak (or stewing steak)

Optional sauces:
Tomato ketchup
Brown sauce
Worcester sauce
Soy sauce
Few drops of tabasco sauce

Garlic powder (optional)
Pinch of dried herbs (optional)
1 small packet instant mashed potatoes – use the amount specified in the instructions on the packet
½ oz (12g) butter or margarine
Hot water
1 oz (25g) grated cheese (optional)
1 tomato (optional)

Empty the meat into a saucepan and bring it gently to the boil, stirring well. Add your chosen sauces and garlic powder and herbs. Simmer for 2 to 3 minutes until really hot.

Make up the instant mashed potato as directed on the packet using the butter and hot water and add most of the grated cheese (saving a little for the top).

Pour the meat mixture into an oven-proof dish, top with the mashed potato, and sprinkle with the remainder of the cheese and/or sliced tomato if used. Dot with a little butter or margarine. Cook under a hot grill, until golden brown (2 to 3 minutes).

POTATO BOLOGNESE

Serves 1

For those of you who don't like pasta, or want a change from spaghetti. Use either traditional or quick Bolognese sauce.

Preparation and cooking time: 45 minutes (traditional)
or 25 minutes (quick).

Traditional Bolognese sauce (see page 210) or
  Quick Bolognese sauce (see page 211)
3–4 potatoes
Knob of butter
1 oz (25g) grated cheese (or Parmesan cheese)

TRADITIONAL METHOD

Prepare the Bolognese sauce and leave to simmer.

Peel and slice the potatoes thickly and cook in boiling, salted water for 10 minutes, until soft (see page 107).

Drain and mash the potatoes with the butter, beating them well. Pile them onto a hot dish, forming them into a border or 'nest'. Pour the Bolognese sauce into the potato nest.

Serve with grated or Parmesan cheese.

QUICK METHOD

Peel and cook the potatoes first, preparing the quick sauce while the potatoes are cooking. Then prepare the dish as above in the traditional method.

BEEF CURRY

A change from the Indian take-away. This is a medium-hot curry, and is easier to prepare for two or more people, as very small amounts tend to dry up during cooking. Why not try double the quantity?

Serve with plain boiled rice (see page 118), poppadums and some side dishes (see opposite).

Preparation and cooking time: 1 hour 50 minutes – 2 hours 50 minutes.

(For one person cook 4 oz stewing beef for 1 hour 30 minutes; for 2 people cook 8 oz stewing beef for about 2 hours; for larger quantities cook for 2 hours 30 minutes.)

1 onion
4–6 oz (100–175g) stewing beef
Little cooking oil (for frying)
2 level tsp curry powder (more or less according to taste)
1 small apple (preferably a cooker)
1 tomato
½ stock cube and 1 cup (¼ pt/150ml) boiling water (or ½ a 295g can mulligatawny soup)
2 tsp sultanas
1 tsp sugar
2 tsp pickle or chutney

Peel and slice the onion. Cut the beef into 1 in (2.5cm) cubes.

Heat the oil in a medium-sized saucepan and fry the onion gently, to soften it, for 3 to 5 minutes. Add the beef and fry for a further 5 minutes, until the meat is browned. Sprinkle the curry powder over the meat, and stir for a few minutes over a medium heat.

Peel and chop the apple, wash and chop the tomato, and add both to the meat and continue frying for 3 to 4 minutes, stirring gently.

Dissolve the stock cube in 1 cup of boiling water and add the stock to the meat, or add the mulligatawny soup. Wash and drain the sultanas. Add them to the curry with the sugar and pickle or chutney. Stir well and simmer gently, with the lid on, stirring occasionally, for 1½ to 2½ hours (the longer time is needed for larger quantities) until the meat is tender.

Side Dishes for Curries
Salted nuts
Chopped green peppers
Plain yoghurt
Sliced onions
Sliced banana (sprinkle with lemon juice to keep it white)
Chopped apple (sprinkle with lemon juice to keep it white)
Chopped cucumber
Chopped, hard-boiled egg
Washed, drained sultanas
Mango chutney
Desiccated coconut

POPPADUMS

Great fun to cook. Buy a packet of Indian poppadums, on sale at large supermarkets.

Heat 3–4 tbsp cooking oil in a frying pan over a medium heat (enough to cover the base of the pan). When the oil is hot float a poppadum on top, and it will puff up immediately, only taking a few moments to cook. Remove it carefully and leave it to drain on kitchen paper while cooking the next poppadum. Do not let the fat get too hot, or it will get smoky and burn.

HOME-MADE BEEFBURGERS
Serves 1

These are quite a change from the commercially-produced beefburgers. You can make them bun-sized or 'half pounders'. Buy a good quality mince, as finely chopped as possible.

Serve in soft bread rolls (these are traditionally lightly toasted on one side) with tomato or barbecue sauce, or with potatoes, vegetables or a salad.

Preparation and cooking time: 20–25 minutes according to size.

½ small onion
4–8 oz (125–225g) minced beef, according to appetite
Salt and pepper
Pinch of dried herbs
Worcester (or tabasco) sauce
Little beaten egg (or egg yolk)
Little oil (for frying)

Peel and finely chop the onion, and mix well in a bowl with the minced beef, using a fork. Mix in the salt, pepper, herbs and sauce and bind together with a little egg. The mixture should be wet enough so the ingredients mould together, but not soggy. Divide this into 2 portions, shape each into a ball, and then flatten into a circle, about ¾ in (2cm) thick.

Heat the oil in a frying pan over a medium heat. Put the beefburgers carefully in the pan, and fry for 10 to 15 minutes, according to size, turning occasionally to cook both sides. Do not have the heat too high, as the beefburgers need to cook right through to the middle without burning the outside.

BOEUF STROGANOFF
Serves 2

Absolutely delicious, rather expensive and very impressive if you have a special friend to dinner. Serve with plain boiled rice, noodles or new potatoes, and a salad.

Preparation and cooking time: 25 minutes.

1 cup plain boiled rice (or 2 cups noodles or 3–6 new potatoes)
8 oz (225g) fillet (or rump) steak
1 medium onion
1 oz (25g) butter (or little cooking oil)
4 oz (100g) mushrooms
1 small green pepper
Salt and pepper
Garlic powder
3–4 tbsp soured cream (or double cream or plain yoghurt)
Chopped parsley

Cook the rice, noodles or scrubbed new potatoes in boiling salted water. Cut the steak into thin strips: 2 in (5cm) long by ½ in (1cm) wide by ¼ in (0.5cm) thick. Peel and chop the onion finely and fry in half the oil or butter in a frying pan or wok, until soft (2 to 3 minutes). Wash and slice the mushrooms. Wash the pepper, remove its core and seeds, and cut it into strips. Add the mushrooms and the pepper to the frying pan and fry gently for a further 4 to 5 minutes.

Remove all the vegetables from the pan and place onto a plate. Melt the remaining butter or oil in the pan, then add the steak strips and fry for 3 to 4 minutes, turning frequently so that they cook evenly. Return the onion, pepper and mushrooms to the pan. Add the salt, pepper and garlic powder. Gently stir in the cream or yoghurt and mix well. Heat carefully until piping hot, but try not to let the sauce boil. Sprinkle with chopped parsley if you want it to look impressive. Drain the rice, noodles or potatoes and serve at once.

177

CHILLI CON CARNE

Serves 1

This is another dish which is easier to make in slightly larger quantities than are given below, so if possible double the ingredients and cook for 2 people. You can use mince or stewing steak. If using raw kidney beans be very careful: they must be fast boiled in water for half an hour before using in this recipe, otherwise they could be poisonous.

Preparation and cooking time: 2 hours 55 minutes (if using stewing steak) 1 hour 25 minutes (if using mince).

1 small onion
1 clove of garlic (or little garlic powder)
Little cooking oil
½ oz (12g) butter
1 rasher of bacon (or bacon trimmings)
4 oz (100g) stewing steak (or minced beef)
1 tbsp tomato purée (or ketchup)
1 cup water
Salt and pepper
½ level tsp chilli powder
½ small (7.5 oz/213g size) can cooked red kidney beans or 4 oz
    (100g) pre-cooked kidney beans (boiled for half an hour in
    fast boiling water, then drained)
Few drops of tabasco sauce (optional)

Peel and chop the onion and garlic. Put the oil and butter into a saucepan. Add the onion and fry gently until soft (2 to 3 minutes). Cut the bacon into small pieces. Add the bacon and stewing steak (or mince) to the pan and fry until browned, stirring so that it cooks evenly. Add the tomato purée (or ketchup), water, salt, pepper and chilli powder. Bring to the boil. Cover, lower the heat and leave to simmer for 1 hour (if using mince) or for 2½ hours (if using stewing steak), stirring occasionally (adding a little extra water if it gets too dry). Add the kidney beans. Simmer for a further 10 minutes. Taste (but be careful not to burn your tongue) and add tabasco sauce if liked. Serve hot.

GRILLED (OR FRIED) STEAK   *Serves 1*

A very special treat! Cheaper 'tenderised' steak can be bought in the supermarket. This is often good value, as it cooks very much like the more expensive cuts. You can buy a smaller amount of steak and add sausages, lamb's kidneys or beefburgers to your meal. Grilled tomatoes and mushrooms are also tasty with steak (see below). Serve with jacket spuds, sauté potatoes, boiled potatoes, baked stuffed potatoes or bread rolls, and a salad or peas. Prepare the vegetables before cooking the meat, as steak is best eaten immediately it is ready. To cook the vegetables see Chapter 5. Grilling is the best way to cook steak, but it can be fried too.

CUTS OF BEEF TO CHOOSE
Minute
Very thin slices, good for a steak sandwich.

Rump
Good flavour, quite lean. Cut it into portions at least ¾ in (2cm) thick.

Sirloin
Very tender, with some fat. Cut as rump.

Fillet
Very tender, very expensive! Cut into even thicker portions 1–1½ in (2.5–3.75cm) thick so that it stays juicy during cooking.

Tournedos
Fillet steak tied into rounds by the butcher; very, very expensive.

Preparation time: 2–3 minutes.
Cooking time: see method.

179

Allow 6–8 oz (175–225g) steak per serving
A little cooking oil (or butter)

GRILLED

Heat the grill. Put the steak on the greased grid of the grill pan and brush or wipe it with the oil or butter. Cook on one side, then turn it over carefully (do not stab the meat). Brush or wipe the second side with the oil or butter and cook to suit your taste:

Minute steak
1 minute cooking on each side.

'Rare' steak
2–4 minutes each side, depending on thickness.

Medium steak
Cook as 'rare', then lower the heat for a further 3–4 minutes each side.

Well done steak
Cook as 'rare', then lower the heat for a further 4–5 minutes each side.

FRIED

Heat the frying pan gently. Put a little oil or fat in the pan. Add the steak, and cook over a medium-high heat, as for grilled steak above. Serve immediately with chosen vegetables.

Sausages and beefburgers can be cooked with the steak. Thick sausages may need a bit longer to cook than the steak, so put them under the grill or in the frying pan first, then add the steak. (See page 133.) Cut lamb's kidney in half lengthways, remove the fatty 'core', and grill or fry for 3 to 5 minutes, with the steak. Cut tomatoes in half and grill under the steak in the grill pan, or fry in the frying pan with the meat, for 3 to 5 minutes. Mushrooms are best cooked in the bottom of the grill pan with a little butter, with the meat juices dripping onto them, or they can be fried in the frying pan with the steak. They will take from 3 to 5 minutes, according to size.

MOORLAND PASTIES
Makes 4

A quickly cooked meat and vegetable pastry, filled with whatever's left in the fridge. It's tasty hot or cold, and can be served as part of a main meal or in a packed lunch. You can use lamb, pork, chicken or ham instead of the beef if you have any left over from a previous meal.

Preparation and cooking time: 40–45 minutes.

8 oz (250g) homemade (see page 37) or bought shortcrust
   pastry
4 oz (100g) cooked beef
1 medium onion
2 medium-sized boiled potatoes
3–4 tbsp cooked mixed vegetables – carrots, swede, peas,
   cauliflower, broccoli, etc.
Salt, pepper, mixed herbs
Dash of Worcester sauce or 1 tbsp pickle or chutney
   (optional)
1 tbsp gravy, brown sauce or tomato ketchup (for mixing)
Little milk (for brushing)

Heat the oven to 400°F/200°C/Gas Mark 6–7. Roll the pastry out to approximately ¼ in (0.5cm) thick and cut out 4 rounds using a large saucer or tea-plate.

    Chop or mince the beef and put into a bowl. Chop finely or mince the onion and add to the beef. Dice the potatoes, chop the vegetables (not too small), and stir into the beef mixture. Season well, adding herbs, pickles and sauces to taste, adding a little gravy if necessary to bind the mixture together.

Divide the filling between the pastry rounds, brush the edges with milk and bring the pastry edges together to form pasties. Press tightly to seal and flute the edges. Put onto a baking sheet, brush with milk and prick steam holes on each side. Bake for 20 minutes, until the pastry is lightly browned, reducing the oven heat after 10 minutes to 350°F/180°C/Gas Mark 4–5 if the pastry seems to be getting too brown (you must allow time to cook the filling thoroughly, not just warm it through).

10
Chicken

Fresh and frozen chicken (whole, chicken joints, boneless or fillets) are extremely good value for money. There is very little waste, as all the scraps can be eaten cold or used up in sandwiches or risotto.

Chicken must be thoroughly defrosted before you start cooking, by leaving the chicken on a plate at room temperature for several hours, according to the instructions on the packet. You can hurry the defrosting process by putting the nearly-thawed chicken in a bowl of cold (not hot) water to get rid of all the ice crystals. Chicken defrosted too quickly in hot water will be tough when cooked. If chicken is not completely thawed before cooking it may not cook right through and any bacteria present will not be destroyed and could make you ill.

Chicken must be cooked thoroughly too. The juices should run clear, not tinged with pink, when pierced with a knife at the thickest part of the joint.

There are also lots of delicious, ready-prepared chicken dishes available at supermarkets, both chilled and frozen. These must be defrosted and cooked strictly according to the instructions on the packet.

FRIED CHICKEN   *Serves 1*

A quick and easy dinner, served with new or sauté potatoes, peas or a green salad. It is also tasty when eaten with new bread rolls and butter.

Preparation and cooking time: 20–22 minutes plus defrosting time.

1 chicken breast or leg joint – 6–8 oz (175–225g) according to your appetite
Little oil and a knob of butter (for frying)

Defrost the chicken for several hours at room temperature according to the instructions on the packet. (See page 183.) Wash the chicken pieces and dry them on kitchen paper.

Heat the oil and butter in a frying pan over a moderate heat, add the chicken and fry it gently for 15 to 20 minutes, according to size, turning it occasionally so that it browns on both sides. If the chicken seems to be getting too brown, lower the heat, but continue cooking, as the chicken needs to cook right through. Remove from the pan, and drain on kitchen paper. Serve hot or cold.

184

CHICKEN WITH SWEETCORN
Serves 2

The sweetcorn and potato sauce turns fried chicken into a complete meal. Serve with rice or potatoes.

Preparation and cooking time: 25–30 minutes plus defrosting time.

2 chicken breasts or leg joints – each joint 6–8 oz (175–225g) according to your appetite
Little oil and knob of butter (for frying)
1 onion
1 can (10 oz/284g) new potatoes
½ can (11½ oz/329g size) sweetcorn
½ oz (12g) butter
2 tsp flour
1 cup (5 fl oz/150ml) milk
Salt and pepper

Defrost the chicken for several hours at room temperature. (See page 183.)

Fry the chicken in the oil and butter, turning occasionally, for 15 to 20 minutes, until cooked and golden brown (see page 184).

Make the sauce while the chicken is frying. Peel and slice the onion. Drain the potatoes and sweetcorn. Melt the butter in a saucepan over a moderate heat, and fry the onion gently for 2 to 3 minutes. Add the potatoes and cook for a further 5 minutes, stirring gently.

Add the sweetcorn and mix well. Stir in the flour, and cook for 2 to 3 minutes. Remove from the heat, and gradually add the milk. Return to the heat and bring to the boil, stirring until the sauce thickens. Simmer for a few minutes, stirring gently, trying not to break up the potatoes. Season the sauce with the salt and pepper. Put the chicken onto a warm serving dish, cover with the sauce and serve at once.

CHICKEN IN TOMATO AND MUSHROOM SAUCE

Serves 1

Fried chicken served in a tasty sauce. This dish is good with boiled rice or potatoes which can be cooked while the chicken is frying.

Preparation and cooking time: 40 minutes plus defrosting time.

1 chicken breast or leg joint – 6–8 oz (175–225g) according to your appetite
Little oil and knob of butter (for frying)
½ small onion
2–3 mushrooms
½ stock cube
½ cup hot water
2 tsp tomato purée (or tomato ketchup)
Pinch of dried mixed herbs
Salt and pepper
Pinch of garlic powder

Defrost the chicken for several hours at room temperature. (See page 183.)

Heat the oil and butter in a frying pan over a moderate heat, and fry the chicken for 15 to 20 minutes, turning occasionally, until cooked through and golden brown (see page 184). Remove the chicken to a warm dish and keep hot.

Peel and chop the onion, put it into the oil in the frying pan and fry gently for 2 to 3 minutes, until soft. Wash and slice the mushrooms, and add to the onion. Dissolve the stock cube in the hot water, add to the onion in the pan, bring to the boil, stirring all the time, then reduce the heat and cook for a further 5 minutes. Add the tomato purée, herbs, seasoning, and garlic powder, and continue cooking for another 4 to 5 minutes – the sauce should now be thick and will coat the chicken. Pour the sauce over the chicken.

186

ROAST CHICKEN PIECES   *Serves 1*

A quick and economical roast dinner. The chicken pieces are cooked in a roasting tin in the oven in the same way as a whole roast chicken, and can be served with thyme and parsley stuffing, sausages, bread sauce, apple sauce, roast potatoes and vegetables to make a traditional roast dinner.

Preparation and cooking time: 35–45 minutes according to size (plus defrosting time).

**Quarter (6–8 oz/175–225g) of a chicken (breast or leg) or 2
   chicken pieces
2 tsp oil and ½ oz (12g) butter (for cooking)
Dried herbs (optional)
Cooking foil**

Defrost the chicken thoroughly for several hours at room temperature. (See page 183.)

Heat the oven at 400°F/200°C/Gas Mark 6–7. Rub the chicken with the oil and dot with the butter. Sprinkle with herbs, if liked. Place in a well-greased roasting tin and cover with cooking foil.

Roast for 30 to 40 minutes, according to the size of the chicken pieces, until the juices run clear (not pink) when tested with a fork. (If still pink, cook for a few more minutes.) Remove the foil for the last 10 minutes of cooking time to brown the chicken. Chipolata sausages, roast potatoes and parsnips can be cooked round the chicken pieces. Remove the chicken, and the sausages, potatoes and parsnips (if used) from the tin, and keep warm. Use the juices left in the roasting tin to make the gravy (see page 230).

187

EASY CHICKEN CASSEROLE   *Serves 2*

Make this for 2 people, otherwise the sauce will dry up before the chicken is cooked. It can be prepared very quickly and popped into the oven. Put a couple of jacket potatoes to cook in the oven with it, and you have a complete meal.

Preparation and cooking time: 1 hour 10 minutes plus defrosting time.

2 chicken breast or leg joints – each joint 6–8 oz (175–225g) according to your appetite
Little oil (for frying)
4 oz (100–125g) can or frozen mixed vegetables
1 small can (10.4 oz/295g) condensed chicken soup
Salt and pepper
Garlic powder or paste (optional)

Defrost the chicken for several hours at room temperature. (See page 183.) Heat the oil in a frying pan over a moderate heat, and fry the chicken for 5 minutes, turning so that it browns on all sides. Remove the chicken. Put it into a casserole with the frozen vegetables. Heat the soup in the pan with the chicken juices, adding the seasoning and garlic. Pour this sauce over the chicken. Cover with a lid, and cook for about an hour, until the chicken is tender, either in a moderate oven (350°F/180°C/Gas Mark 4) or over a very low heat on top of the stove.

CHICKEN CURRY   *Serves 1*

Defrost the chicken joint at room temperature. (See page 183.) Make the curry using the recipe given for beef curry (on page 174), substituting the chicken joint for the stewing beef. Chicken cooks more quickly than stewing beef, so the curry need only be simmered for about an hour. Serve with boiled rice (see page 118) and curry side dishes as suggested on page 175.

HAWAIIAN CHICKEN
Serves 1

Cook half the tin of pineapple with the chicken, then eat the rest for pudding, with ice-cream, cream or yoghurt. Serve the Hawaiian chicken with new or sauté potatoes, or potato castles, and green beans or peas.

Preparation and cooking time: 40 minutes plus defrosting time.

1 chicken joint (6–8 oz/175–225g)
1 tsp oil and knob of butter (for cooking)
½ small can (7¾ oz/220g size) pineapple pieces, chunks or slices in syrup
1 tsp flour or cornflour
1 tsp soy sauce
1 tsp Worcester sauce

Defrost the chicken for several hours at room temperature (see page 183).

Heat the oil and butter in a frying pan, and fry the chicken over a moderate heat for 10 minutes, turning occasionally so that it browns on all sides. Remove from the pan for a few minutes.

Drain the pineapple, saving the syrup. Mix the flour (or cornflour) into a smooth paste with a little of the syrup. Add the remainder of the syrup and stir this liquid into the juices in the frying pan, stirring until the sauce thickens. Return the chicken to the pan, add the pineapple pieces, and pour the soy sauce and Worcester sauce over the chicken. Stir well, then lower the heat and simmer for 15 minutes, stirring occasionally.

CHICKEN IN WINE
Serves 1

This can be made with a chicken joint on the bone, but is super made with boneless chicken breast or filleted turkey, according to your taste and pocket. Serve with new potatoes and peas.

Preparation and cooking time: 45–60 minutes plus defrosting time (chicken on the bone takes the longest time).

1 chicken joint (6–8 oz/175–225g), boneless chicken breast or slice of turkey fillet
1 small onion
1 stock cube – preferably chicken flavour
½ cup hot water
1 tsp oil and knob of butter
1 wine glass of white wine (or cider)
½ tsp herbs
Salt and pepper
1 tsp flour (or cornflour)

Defrost the chicken thoroughly for several hours at room temperature (see page 183). Peel and finely chop the onion. Dissolve the stock cube in the ½ cup of hot water. Heat the oil and butter over a moderate heat, in a casserole or thick saucepan, and fry the chicken gently for a few minutes, turning it so that it browns on all sides. Remove from the pan. Add the onion to the pan, and stir over the moderate heat for a few minutes to soften.

Pour most of the wine (or cider) onto the onion, stir well and allow to bubble for a minute. Return the chicken to the sauce. Stir in the stock, herbs, salt and pepper (according to taste). Cover the pan, and simmer very gently for 30–45 minutes, until the chicken is tender. Mix the flour with the rest of the wine (or cider) to make a smooth paste, and gradually stir this into the chicken sauce, until it has thickened a little. Serve hot.

SPANISH CHICKEN

Serves 1

An easy dish to make which uses up any left-over, cooked chicken you may have. Serve with French bread and butter or as part of a buffet with other salads.

Preparation and cooking time: 20–35 minutes, according to the type of rice used (it's even quicker if you use up pre-cooked rice and serve the dish cold).

2–3 oz (50–75g) dry Patna or brown rice or 4–6 oz (100–150g/1 cup) cooked rice
Pinch of saffron (optional)
3–4 oz (75–100g) cooked chicken
1–2 spring onions or ½ small onion
1–2 tbsp canned sweetcorn
1–2 tsp vinaigrette dressing
1 tbsp mayonnaise
Few black or green olives
1–2 tsp flaked almonds or pine kernels
Salt, black pepper, cayenne or paprika pepper

Rinse the raw rice thoroughly in several pans of cold water to get rid of the starch, then cook the rice in a pan of boiling water, with the saffron if used, for 10 to 12 minutes for Patna rice or 20 to 25 minutes for brown rice (or as directed on the packet), until the rice is cooked *al dente*, not mushy.

While the rice is cooking, slice the chicken into strips. Wash and slice the spring onions or finely chop the onion. Drain the sweetcorn.

Drain the rice well, tip into a bowl and mix the vinaigrette dressing with the rice. Mix the chicken, onion and sweetcorn into the rice, stir in the mayonnaise and season to taste. Pile the rice mixture onto a serving dish, garnish with olives and sprinkle with sliced almonds or pine kernels.

CHINESE CHICKEN
Serves 3–4

This dish can be made with raw or cooked chicken. Serve with ribbon noodles or tagliatelle.

Preparation and cooking time: 30 minutes (cooked chicken)
40 minutes (raw chicken)

12 oz (350g) boned chicken (raw or cold roast meat)
2 onions
2 cloves of garlic or ½ tsp garlic powder
4 oz (100g) mushrooms
¼ cucumber
2 eating apples
1 red or green pepper (or half of each colour)
2 oz (50g) butter with 1 tbsp vegetable oil (for frying)
4 oz (100g/1 large cup) cooked rice

Sweet and sour sauce:
1 level tbsp cornflour
1 dsp soy sauce
3 tbsp vinegar
2 tbsp sugar or honey
¼ pt (150ml) chicken stock or gravy

Slice the chicken into bite-sized chunks or strips. Peel and slice the onions and garlic. Wash and slice the mushrooms. Wash and dice the cucumber. Wash, core and slice the apples (peel them if you prefer). Wash and chop or slice the pepper.

Heat the butter and oil in a wok or large frying pan over a moderate heat, and fry the raw chicken, if used, for 4 to 5 minutes until golden. Remove it from the pan with a slotted spoon. Add a little more butter and oil to the pan if needed and fry the onion and garlic gently for 3 to 4 minutes until soft. Add the mushrooms, apples, cucumber and pepper and continue stir frying for a further 5 minutes until all the vegetables are softened. Add the cooked chicken or the cold roast chicken, cover the pan and cook gently for a further 5 minutes until the chicken is cooked and the vegetables are tender but not soggy.

Make the sauce while the vegetables are cooking. Put the cornflour into a small pan and mix to a smooth paste with the soy sauce and vinegar. Add the sugar, honey and the stock or thin gravy. Put the pan over a moderate heat and bring to the boil, stirring all the time, then simmer for 2 to 3 minutes until the sauce thickens and becomes transparent.

Stir the cooked rice into the chicken and vegetable mixture, and stir fry for a minute until really hot. Tip the mixture onto a warm serving dish or serve straight from the pan. Pour the hot sweet and sour sauce over the top and sprinkle with washed finely snipped parsley if liked.

LAMB COUNTER

11
Lamb

Leg and shoulder are the dearest joints of lamb, with leg costing more than shoulder. These are strictly 'special occasion' meals, and are explained under 'Sunday Lunch Dishes' in Chapter 14. Lamb chops (loin, chump and leg chops are the big ones; cutlets are the small ones) make a quickly-cooked, tasty meal, but are also quite expensive. Stewing lamb (middle and best end of lamb, scrag end and breast of lamb) is much cheaper. These cuts of lamb are stewed with the meat left on the bone (so you buy more weight of meat than you do with beef) but need long, slow cooking. They make really delicious meals fairly cheaply. Breast of lamb can be boned, stuffed, rolled and roasted, and makes a very cheap and tasty Sunday dinner.

LAMB CHOPS – GRILLED OR FRIED   *Serves 1*

Choose lean chops, but remember that lamb is basically a fatty kind of meat, and the fat gives the meat a good flavour. Chump and loin chops are larger than cutlets. Very small cutlets are sold in some supermarkets as 'breakfast chops', so decide how hungry you are feeling when you choose your chop.

Sausages, lamb's kidney or beefburgers can be cooked with the chops. Grill or fry the sausages first as they take longer to cook than the lamb. Tomatoes, mushrooms, new potatoes and peas go well with it too. Traditionally mint sauce (see page 234), mint jelly, redcurrant jelly or onion sauce (see page 232) are served with lamb.

Preparation and cooking time: 12–17 minutes.

1 chump or loin chop or 1–2 lamb cutlets
Little oil

GRILLED

Heat the grill. Brush or rub both sides of the chop with a smear of the oil. Place the chop on the greased grid of the grill pan and grill for 8 to 10 minutes, according to its size and your taste, turning the meat so that it browns evenly on both sides. Lamb is traditionally served pink and underdone in the middle, and brown and crispy on the outside, but cook the chops how you like them.

FRIED

Heat a little oil in a frying pan over a medium heat. Put the chops in the pan and fry, turning several times, for 8 to 10 minutes, until the chops are brown and crispy and cooked according to taste.

OVEN CHOP

A tasty dinner, served with a jacket potato which can cook in the oven with the casserole. This dish is equally good made with a pork chop.

Preparation and cooking time: 50–55 minutes.

1 small onion
3–4 mushrooms
½ tbsp oil (for frying)
1 chump or loin chop
½ small (8 oz/230g size) can tomatoes
Salt and pepper
Pinch of herbs

Peel and slice the onion. Wash and slice the mushrooms. Heat the oil in a frying pan over a medium heat. Fry the onion for 3 to 4 minutes to soften it. Add the chop to the pan, and cook on both sides for a few minutes, to brown. Add the mushrooms and cook for another minute. Put the chop into a casserole or oven-proof dish and pour the onion and mushrooms on the top.

Heat the tomatoes in the frying pan with the meat juices. Add these to the casserole, with the salt, pepper and herbs. Cover with a lid or cooking foil. Bake in a hot oven (400°F/200°C/Gas Mark 6) for 45 minutes, removing the lid for the last 15 minutes, to reduce the sauce to make it thicker.

If serving with a jacket potato, scrub and prick the potato, and cook it in boiling water for 10 minutes. Drain the potato. Lift it out carefully and put it into the oven to bake with the casserole for 30 to 45 minutes, according to size.

IRISH STEW WITH DUMPLINGS   *Serves 2*

This should satisfy even the hungriest Irishman. It makes a substantial meal on its own but can be served with extra potatoes or bread rolls, and a green vegetable.

Preparation and cooking time: 2 hours 20 minutes – 2 hours 50 minutes.

¾–1 lb (350–450g) middle neck or scrag end of lamb
2 onions
2 carrots
1–2 potatoes
1 tbsp oil (for frying)
1 stock cube
2–3 cups boiling water
½ tsp mixed herbs
Salt and pepper

For the dumplings:
4 oz (100g/4 heaped tbsp) self-raising flour
Salt and pepper
2 oz (50g/2 tbsp) shredded suet

For thicker gravy:
1 tbsp gravy granules
    or 2 tsp flour (or cornflour) and 1 tsp gravy flavouring powder
1 tbsp cold water, sherry, beer or wine

Cut the lamb into pieces suitable for serving. Trim off any large pieces of fat. Peel and slice the onions and carrots. Peel the potatoes and cut them into chunks.

Heat the oil in a large saucepan. Fry the onion and carrots over a medium heat for 3–4 minutes, stirring occasionally. Add the pieces of meat and fry for a further 2–3 minutes, trying to brown all the sides of the meat. Add the potato chunks. Dissolve the stock cube in 1 cup of boiling water, and pour it over the meat, adding enough extra water to

197

cover the meat and vegetables. Add the herbs, salt and pepper. Stir gently and bring back to the boil, then reduce the heat and simmer over a very low heat for 1½ hours, with the lid on.

Make the dumplings by mixing together the self-raising flour, salt, pepper and suet. Add just enough cold water to make a dough – like very soft putty or plasticine. Divide this into 4 pieces and shape into dumplings. Carefully lower the dumplings into the stew and cook for a further 25–30 minutes, making sure the liquid is boiling gently all the time (keep the lid on the pan as much as possible, without letting it boil over).

If the gravy needs to be thicker, mix the gravy granules or the flour (or cornflour) and gravy flavouring powder into a smooth paste with a little cold water, sherry, wine or beer. Stir it into the stew, stirring well while the gravy thickens.

REAL LANCASHIRE HOT POT   *Serves 2*
This dish may also be eaten by Yorkshiremen, and those from other lesser counties!

Preparation and cooking time: 2 hours 15 minutes.

12–16 oz (350–450g) best end or middle neck of lamb
1 lamb's kidney
2 onions
1 carrot
1 very small turnip (optional)
3 or 4 potatoes, total weight 1 lb (450g)
1 tbsp oil (for frying)
1 stock cube
2 cups (½ pt/300ml) approx. boiling water
2 tsp flour or cornflour
Salt and pepper
Pinch of dried herbs
Knob of butter

Cut the lamb into pieces suitable for serving. Skin the kidney, cut in half lengthways, cut out the white fatty core and cut the kidney into pieces. Peel and slice the onions, carrot and turnip (if used). Peel and slice the potatoes and cut into thick slices (½ in/1.25cm).

Heat the oil in a frying pan, and brown the lamb pieces, over a medium heat, turning them so that they cook on all sides. Brown the kidney, and arrange all the meat in a casserole or oven-proof dish. Fry the onion in the pan for 3 to 4 minutes, to soften it. Add the sliced carrot and turnip (if used) and continue to fry gently, stirring all the time, for a further 3 minutes.

Add the vegetables to the meat in the casserole. Dissolve the stock cube in 2 cups of boiling water. Sprinkle the flour over the remaining juices in the frying pan, and stir. Gradually stir in the stock, stirring hard to make a smooth gravy and adding the salt, pepper and herbs. Pour the gravy over the meat in the casserole, to cover the meat and vegetables.

Then cover the meat with a thick layer of potato slices, placing them so that they overlap and form a thick crust. Dot with the butter. Cover with a lid or piece of tight-fitting foil, and cook in a moderate oven (325°F/170°C/Gas Mark 3–4) for 1½–2 hours, removing the lid for the last half hour of cooking time, to brown the top. If the top does not seem to be getting crispy enough, either increase the oven heat to 400°F/200°C/Gas Mark 6–7, or pop the casserole dish under a hot grill for a few minutes.

If you have to cook the casserole on top of the stove because an oven is not available, simmer the casserole very gently for 1½ to 2 hours, then brown the potato topping under the grill as described above.

12
Pork

Pork is quite a 'good buy', being generally cheaper than beef or the better cuts of lamb. It is a rich meat, so is filling too. It is important that pork is cooked thoroughly; it is better over-cooked than underdone, and must never, ever, be served pink, as rare pork can make you ill with food poisoning. The meat must look pale-coloured, right through. Cold roast pork should not be re-heated; eat it cold if you have any left over. If you are heating cooked pork dishes in a sauce, make sure this pork is really re-cooked right through to kill any bacteria, not just warmed up. Leg, shoulder and loin of pork are the more expensive cuts, and make far too much for one person. Details of how to cook them are given under 'Sunday Lunch Dishes', Chapter 14. Chops, spare ribs and belly are more suitable and economical for small quantities, so here are some ideas!

200

PORK CHOP – GRILLED OR FRIED   *Serves 1*

Quick and easy, and not too expensive. Tastes good with
sauté potatoes, a grilled or fried tomato, pineapple rings or a
spoonful of apple sauce. Pork is better grilled, as it can be a
bit fatty, but frying is quite acceptable if you don't have a
grill. Whichever way you choose to cook it, make sure it is
cooked thoroughly, the juices must run clear, not pink, and
the meat must be pale-coloured right through. Undercooked
pork can make you ill, so do cook it thoroughly.

Preparation and cooking time: 14–16 minutes.

1 pork chop
Little oil or butter
½ tsp dried mixed herbs (or dried sage)
1 tomato (or 1–2 pineapple rings or 1 tbsp apple sauce)
Cooked, cold, boiled potatoes to sauté

Heat the grill or heat a frying pan over a moderate heat with
a smear of oil. Rub both sides of the chop with the oil or
butter, sprinkle with the herbs. Either put the chop under the
hot grill, turning frequently, until brown and crispy, 12 to 15
minutes (lowering the heat if the chop starts getting too
brown); or, put the chop into the hot frying pan and fry over
a moderate heat for 12 to 15 minutes, turning frequently,
until brown and cooked thoroughly.

ACCOMPANIMENTS

Cut the tomato in half, dot with butter and put under the grill
or into the frying pan for the last 3 to 4 minutes of cooking
time; or, put the pineapple slices on top of the chop under
the grill or in the frying pan for 1 to 2 minutes to warm
slightly; or, prepare the apple sauce in advance from the
recipe on page 233 (or use apple sauce from a jar or can from
the supermarket). Fry the sauté potatoes while the chop is
cooking (see page 109). If you have only one frying pan you
can cook them in the pan with the chop.

MUSTARD-GLAZED PORK CHOP

Serves 1

A tangy hot grilled chop. Serve with new or sauté potatoes and a green vegetable.

Preparation and cooking time: 17–20 minutes.

1 tsp mustard
1 tsp brown sugar
Knob of butter
1 pork chop

Heat the grill.

Mix the mustard, sugar and small knob of butter together in a cup. Spread this mixture over both sides of the chop.

Cook the chop under the hot grill, turning frequently, until brown and crispy (12 to 15 minutes). Lower the heat if the chop gets too brown too quickly. The pork must be cooked right through. The juices must run clear not pink, and the meat must be pale-coloured right through. Under-cooked pork can make you ill, so do cook it thoroughly.

PORK CHOP IN CIDER

Serves 1

Absolutely delicious and the smell of the meal cooking gives you a real appetite.

Preparation and cooking time: 1 hour.

1 tsp cooking oil
½ oz (12g) butter
1 pork chop (preferably a loin chop) or 1 pork steak
1 small onion
1 small cooking apple (you can use an eating apple if necessary)
½–1 cup cider
Salt and pepper
Pinch of dried herbs
1 tbsp cream (you can use plain yoghurt or soured cream)

Heat the oil and butter in a frying pan. Fry both sides of the chop until brown (4 to 5 minutes). Place it in a casserole or an oven-proof dish.

Peel and slice the onion, peel and chop the apple, and fry them together in the frying pan, stirring frequently (4 to 5 minutes) until the onion is soft. Add to the meat in the casserole. Pour enough cider into the casserole so that it covers the meat. Add the salt, pepper and herbs.

Cover, with a lid or piece of foil, and bake in a moderate oven (350°F/180°C/Gas Mark 4–5) for approximately 45 minutes. (If you don't have an oven, this can be cooked very, very, gently in a saucepan on top of the stove for 45 minutes.) Stir in the cream and serve at once.

PORK IN A PACKET

Serves 1

An easy way of cooking pork, without much washing up!

Preparation and cooking time: 1 hour.

1–2 tbsp uncooked long grain rice (or 3 tbsp cold cooked rice)
2 tbsp canned or frozen sweetcorn
2 tbsp frozen peas
1 spring onion (or ½ small onion)
Salt and pepper
Cooking oil
Butter (for greasing the foil)
1 pork chop
1 tsp soy (or Worcester) sauce
1 tbsp cider, white wine or beer

Cook the raw rice in boiling, salted water for 8 to 10 minutes, until just soft. Add the frozen sweetcorn and peas for the last 2 minutes and cook with the rice, or cook by themselves if you are using up cooked rice. (Canned sweetcorn does not need cooking and can be used straight from the can.)

Drain well. Wash and chop the spring onion or peel and chop the onion. Add the onion to the rice mixture, mix well and season with salt and pepper.

Cut a square of cooking foil, large enough to wrap the chop loosely. Grease the foil with the butter, and put the chop in the centre of the foil. Sprinkle with soy or Worcester sauce. Top with the rice mixture and moisten with the cider, wine or beer. Wrap the foil around the chop into a parcel, and put carefully onto a baking tin or dish. Bake in a moderate oven (350°F/180°C/Gas Mark 4–5) for 40 minutes.

CRUNCHY FRIED PORK

Serves 1

Shoulder and belly pork are cheap and tasty. Try to buy thin slices of meat for this dish and flatten them by banging them with a rolling pin. (If you don't have one, use an unopened can of beans etc., wrapped in a polythene bag, to stamp the slices flat.) A crisp green salad or a fresh tomato can accompany this dish.

Preparation and cooking time: 30 minutes.

1–2 potatoes (you can use up cooked potatoes if you have them)
4–6 oz (100–175g/1 or 2 slices) belly or shoulder pork
½ beaten egg (use the rest in scrambled egg)
1 tbsp packet sage and onion stuffing (or 1 tbsp porridge oats)
1 tbsp oil (for frying)
1 onion

Peel the potatoes, cut them in quarters and cook in boiling salted water for 15 minutes, until soft.

Flatten the pork as best you can and, if the pieces are large, cut them into portions. Beat the egg. Dip the pork pieces into the egg, and then toss them in the dry stuffing or porridge oats to coat the meat thoroughly.

Heat the oil in a frying pan. Put the pork pieces carefully into the hot fat and fry both sides of the pork over a medium heat, until brown and cooked right through (about 15 minutes). Put the pork onto a hot dish and keep warm.

Drain the potato when cooked. Cut into dice. Peel and chop the onion and cook in the fat in the frying pan. Add the diced potato and continue cooking until just turning brown and crispy, stirring occasionally. Sprinkle the onion and potatoes over the meat, and serve hot.

SPARE RIBS

Serves 1

Cheap and cheerful. Messy but fun to eat, and filling if you serve with a large jacket potato and plenty of butter. You'll need finger bowls and lots of paper napkins!

Preparation and cooking time: 1 hour 30 minutes – 1 hour 45 minutes.

12–16 oz (350–450g) Chinese-style spare ribs
1 small clove of garlic (or ¼ tsp garlic powder)
1 tbsp soy sauce
1 tsp orange marmalade
1 small onion
Salt and pepper
½ stock cube
½ cup boiling water
1 tsp vinegar

Heat the grill. Put the ribs in the grill pan and brown them under the grill, turning frequently, to seal in the juices. If you don't have a grill, brown the ribs in a frying pan, with a little oil or butter, over a medium heat, for 2 to 3 minutes, turning often. Peel and crush the garlic clove.

Mix the soy sauce, marmalade and garlic, and spread over the ribs. Peel and slice the onion. Put the onion in a casserole or oven-proof dish. Place the ribs on top and season with salt and pepper.

Dissolve the stock cube in ½ cup of boiling water, add the vinegar and pour it all over the ribs. Cover and cook in a hot oven (400°F/200°C/Gas Mark 6–7) for 1¼ to 1½ hours (the longer time for the larger amount). Remove the lid for the last 20 minutes to allow the meat to become crisp. The sauce should be sticky when cooked. The jacket potato can be cooked in the oven with the casserole (see page 109).

13
Pasta

There are numerous shapes of pasta, but they are all cooked in the same way, and most of the different shapes are interchangeable in most recipes, with the exception of the lasagne and cannelloni types.

Spaghetti
Available in various lengths and thicknesses.

Tagliatelle and other Noodle varieties
Sold in strands and bunches.

Fancy shapes
Shells, bows, etc.

Macaroni types
Thicker tubular shapes.

Lasagne
Large flat sheets.

Cannelloni
Usually filled with a tasty stuffing.

Most makes of pasta have the cooking instructions on the packet, and the best advice is to follow these carefully.

Allow approximately 1 cup (3 oz/75g) pasta per serving.

Pasta must be cooked in a large pan of boiling, salted water, with a few drops of cooking oil added to the water to help stop the pasta sticking. Long spaghetti is stood in the pan and pushed down gradually as it softens. Let the water come to the boil, then lower the heat and leave to simmer (without the lid or it will boil over) for 8 to 10 minutes until the pasta is just cooked (*al dente*). Drain well, in a colander preferably, otherwise you risk losing the pasta down the sink. Serve at once.

MACARONI CHEESE   *Serves 1*
This is traditionally made with the thick, tubular macaroni pasta, but it is equally good made with spaghetti or pasta shapes, shells, bows, etc.

Preparation and cooking time: 30 minutes.

1 cup (3 oz/75g) macaroni or chosen pasta (uncooked)
Pinch of salt
½ tsp cooking oil

For the cheese sauce (or use packet sauce mix):
2 oz (50–75g) cheese
2 tsp flour or cornflour

208

1 cup (¼ pt/150ml) milk
½ oz (12g) butter
Salt, pepper, and mustard
Tomato (optional)

For the topping
1 oz (25g) grated cheese

Heat the oven (400°F/200°C/Gas Mark 6). Cook the macaroni or pasta in a large saucepan of boiling water, with a pinch of salt and a few drops of cooking oil, for 10 to 15 minutes, until just cooked (*al dente*).

While the macaroni is cooking, make the cheese sauce either according to the instructions on the packet or by using the following method. Grate the cheese, put the cornflour or flour in a small basin and mix it into paste with a little of the milk. Bring the rest of the milk to the boil in a small pan, then pour it into the flour mixture, stirring all the time. Pour the mixture back into the pan, return to the heat and bring back to the boil, stirring all the time until the sauce thickens. Beat in the butter, salt, pepper, pinch of mustard and the grated cheese.

Drain the macaroni well, and put it into a greased, oven-proof dish. Pour the cheese over the macaroni, and mix slightly. Sprinkle the rest of the cheese on top. Put into the hot oven for 10 minutes, until the cheese is crisp and bubbling, and the macaroni is hot.

This dish can be topped with sliced, fresh tomato and served with a salad. The top can be browned under the grill instead of in the oven, provided the sauce and macaroni are hot when mixed.

TRADITIONAL BOLOGNESE SAUCE   *Serves 1*

This thick meaty sauce can be used with spaghetti, pasta shapes, lasagne or even mashed potato, for a cheap and cheerful dinner.

Preparation and cooking time: 45 minutes.

1 small onion
½ carrot (optional)
½ rasher of bacon (optional)
Clove of garlic or pinch of garlic powder (optional)
2 tsp oil or a little fat (for frying)
3–4 oz (75–100g) minced beef
½ small can (8 oz/230g size) tomatoes or 2 fresh tomatoes
2 tsp tomato purée or tomato ketchup
½ beef stock cube and ½ cup water or ½ small tin
   (10.4 oz/295g size) of tomato soup
Pinch of salt and pepper
Pinch of sugar
Pinch of dried herbs

Peel and chop the onion. Peel and chop or grate the carrot. Chop the bacon. Peel, chop and crush the garlic clove.

Fry the onion and bacon gently in the oil or fat in a saucepan, stirring until the onion is soft (2 to 3 minutes). Add the minced beef and continue cooking, stirring until it is lightly browned. Add the carrot, tinned tomatoes (or chopped fresh ones), tomato purée (or ketchup), stock cube and water (or the soup) stirring well. Add the salt, pepper, sugar and herbs.

Bring to the boil, then lower the heat and simmer, stirring occasionally, for 20 to 30 minutes, until the meat is tender.

QUICK BOLOGNESE SAUCE
Serves 1

Very fast and easy to prepare. Use instead of Bolognese sauce made with fresh minced beef.

Preparation and cooking time: 10 minutes.

1 small tin (7 oz/198g) minced steak
1 or 2 tomatoes (tinned or fresh)
2 tsp tomato purée (or tomato ketchup)
Pinch of garlic powder (optional)
Pinch of salt and pepper
Pinch of sugar
½ tsp dried herbs

Empty the minced steak into a saucepan. Chop the tinned or fresh tomatoes, add to the beef, with the tomato purée (or ketchup), garlic powder, salt, pepper, sugar and herbs. Bring gently to the boil, stirring well, then lower the heat and simmer for 5 minutes, stirring occasionally. Use as traditional Bolognese sauce.

SPAGHETTI BOLOGNESE

Serves 1

Grated Cheddar cheese can be used instead of Parmesan, but a drum of Parmesan keeps for ages in the fridge and goes a long way.

Preparation and cooking time: 25–55 minutes.

Traditional Bolognese Sauce (see page 210) or Quick Bolognese Sauce (see page 211)
3 oz (75g) spaghetti (or 1 cup pasta shells, bows, etc)
½ tsp cooking oil
2 tsp Parmesan cheese (or 1 oz/25g grated Cheddar cheese)

Prepare the Bolognese sauce.

Cook the spaghetti or chosen pasta in a pan of boiling, salted water with ½ tsp cooking oil for 10 to 12 minutes. (If you want to have long spaghetti, stand the bundle of spaghetti in the boiling water and, as it softens, coil it round into the water without breaking.)

Drain the spaghetti and put it onto a hot plate. Pour the sauce into the centre of the spaghetti and sprinkle the cheese on the top. Serve at once.

SPAGHETTI PORK SAVOURY

Serves 1

Belly pork is one of the cheapest cuts of meat you can buy.

Preparation and cooking time: 30 minutes.

1 generous cup (3 oz/75g) pasta – spaghetti, shells, noodles, etc.
Little cooking oil
2 oz (50g/1–2 slices) belly pork
1 onion
2 fresh tomatoes (or 1 small tin (8 oz/230g) tomatoes)
1 oz (25g) Cheddar cheese (or a little Parmesan)

Cook the chosen pasta in a large saucepan of boiling, salted water, with a few drops of cooking oil, for 10 to 12 minutes. Drain and keep hot. Meanwhile, cut the pork into tiny strips, discarding any rind and gristly bits. Peel and chop the onion and chop the fresh tomatoes (if used).

Heat some oil in a frying pan. Add the onion and fry for a few minutes to soften it. Add the pork strips and fry, stirring well, until browned. Add the tomato pieces or tinned tomatoes (not the juice) and stir well.

Cook over a low heat for another 10 minutes, stirring to break up the tomatoes, making a thick, saucy mixture. Grate the cheese. Pour the hot sauce over the spaghetti, and serve at once, sprinkled with the grated cheese.

QUICK LASAGNE
Serves 1

For this recipe you can use the traditional Bolognese sauce (page 210), or else make it up using the first four ingredients listed here. Serve with a green salad.

Preparation and cooking time: 25–30 minutes.

Small tin minced steak (7 oz/198g)
2 tsp tomato purée or tomato ketchup
Pinch of garlic powder
Salt and pepper
3–4 sheets (2 oz/50g) instant lasagne – plain or verdi
½ can (10.4 oz/295g size) condensed chicken (or mushroom) soup mixed with milk or water (enough to fill ¼ of the soup can)
1 oz (25g) cheese – grated or thinly sliced

Put the canned meat into a small saucepan with the tomato purée, garlic, salt and pepper, or put the Bolognese sauce in a pan, and heat gently for 3 to 5 minutes, stirring well, to make a runny sauce (add a little water if needed).

Grease an oven-proof dish – the square foil dishes are excellent for one portion. Put layers of the meat sauce, lasagne sheets and the soup in the dish, ending with a layer of soup. Make sure the lasagne is completely covered with the sauce. Top with the grated or thinly-sliced cheese. Bake for 15 to 20 minutes in an oven (375°F/190°C/Gas Mark 5–6) until the cheese is golden and bubbling.

CHEESY NOODLES

Serves 1

A cheap dish for using up the contents of the cupboard or fridge. Serve with a piece of cheese, tomato or a salad.

Preparation and cooking time: 15 minutes.

1 cup (3 oz/75g) uncooked noodles
1 tsp oil
2 oz (50g) cheese
1 oz (25g) butter
Salt and pepper

Cook the noodles in a large saucepan of boiling, salted water with 1 tsp cooking oil, until just soft (about 7 to 10 minutes).

Grate the cheese, or chop it finely into very small cubes.

Drain the noodles, return to the hot, dry pan and shake for a moment in the pan over the heat, to dry them and keep them hot. Remove from the heat and stir in the cheese and the butter. Season with the salt and pepper and pile onto a hot dish. Serve at once.

CREAMY NUT PASTA   *Serves 1*

A really quick, cheap and cheerful filling snack or supper;
just add a bread roll and green salad if you're very hungry.
You can use any pasta for this dish (spaghetti, shells,
noodles, etc.), but I think tagliatelle is the nicest. A small
helping makes a good starter to a meal.

Preparation and cooking time: 20 minutes.

Salt and pepper
1 tsp cooking oil
3 oz (75g/1 full cup) chosen pasta
1–2 tbsp cream cheese or curd cheese
1–2 tbsp yoghurt or soured cream or double cream
2 tbsp roughly chopped walnuts or cashew nuts
Pinch of paprika pepper

Half fill a large saucepan with hot, salted water, add the oil
and bring to the boil. Throw in the pasta, stir and boil gently
for 5 to 8 minutes until the pasta is cooked *al dente*, but not
soggy. Drain the pasta in a colander or sieve.

Put the cream or curd cheese, yoghurt or cream, and nuts
into the pasta saucepan, and stir over a very low heat until it
is just beginning to melt. Add the pasta to the cream mixture
and stir over a low heat until coated with the cheese mixture.

Season to taste and serve on a warm plate, topped with a
shake of paprika.

NUTTY MUSHROOM PASTA   *Serves 2*

A good 'store cupboard' meal, using up that half tub of yoghurt and that carton of cream cheese left in the fridge. It's much more substantial than it may appear from the recipe – lots of energy-giving carbohydrates for pre-regatta rowing eights! Serve with a crisp mixed salad and garlic bread.

Preparation and cooking time: 35 minutes.

6 oz (150g) pasta shells, bows, spirals, etc
1 tsp cooking oil
1 onion
1–2 cloves of garlic or ¼ tsp garlic paste or powder
4 oz (100g) mushrooms
1–2 tbsp oil (for frying)
2 oz (50g) cream or curd cheese
2 oz (50g) plain yoghurt, soured or double cream
2–3 tbsp roughly chopped walnuts, cashew nuts or pine
    kernels
Handful of fresh parsley
Salt, pepper, shake of paprika pepper

Half fill a large pan with hot, salted water, add 1 tsp cooking oil and bring to the boil. Stir in the pasta and cook for 6 to 8 minutes, until *al dente*, not soggy. Drain well and keep warm.

While the pasta is cooking, peel and finely chop the onions and fresh garlic. Wash and slice the mushrooms. Heat the oil in a pan over a moderate heat and fry the onion and garlic for 4 to 5 minutes, until soft but not brown. Add the mushrooms, cooking gently for a further 4 to 5 minutes, until the vegetables are cooked. Stir in the cream or curd cheese, yoghurt, soured or double cream, and nuts, and heat gently, stirring carefully to make a creamy sauce. Stir the pasta into the creamy mixture, mixing gently to coat the pasta with the sauce and heating thoroughly. Stir in snipped parsley and season to taste. Pile onto a warm serving dish and garnish with a shake of paprika and a little more parsley.

PASTA AND AUBERGINE BAKE   *Serves 2*

An intriguing compromise between lasagne and moussaka
using pasta shapes.

*Preparation and cooking time: 45–50 minutes
              plus draining time for aubergines.*

1 medium-size aubergine
Salt and pepper
**6 oz (150g/2 full cups) dry pasta shapes (shells, bows, etc.);
   use wholemeal pasta if possible**
2–3 tbsp vegetable oil
1 onion
1 clove of fresh garlic or ¼ tsp garlic powder
2 tomatoes (fresh or canned)
1 tbsp tomato purée or ketchup
½ tsp mixed herbs
¼ tsp cayenne pepper (optional)
Few drops of pepper sauce (optional)
¼ tsp sugar
2–3 tbsp juice from canned tomatoes or water
2 oz (50g) Cheddar or Edam cheese, grated
1 tbsp grated Parmesan cheese

Heat the oven to 375°F/190°C/Gas Mark 5–6. Grease an
oven-proof dish or two individual dishes. Trim, wash and
slice the aubergine and put into a colander, sprinkle with
salt, stand the colander on a plate and leave for about an
hour to drain out the bitter juices.

Cook the pasta shapes in boiling, salted water with ½ tsp
vegetable oil until just tender (*al dente*), about 10 minutes, or
as instructed on the packet. Drain the pasta.

Peel and chop the onion and fresh garlic. Wash and chop
the fresh tomatoes. Heat 2 tbsp oil in a frying pan and fry the
onion, garlic and aubergine slices until softened and lightly
golden, turning the slices to colour both sides, adding a little
more oil if needed. Stir in the chopped tomatoes, tomato
purée or ketchup, herbs, cayenne pepper and pepper sauce

218

(if used), sugar, salt and pepper. Add 2 tbsp juice from the canned tomatoes or cold water, and simmer gently for 5 to 10 minutes until the vegetables are soft and the sauce is nice and thick. Add a little more liquid if necessary.

Put a layer of the vegetable mixture into the dishes, then a layer of pasta and then continue to alternate the layers until they are all used up, finishing with a vegetable layer. Sprinkle with grated Cheddar or Edam, and top with Parmesan. Bake for 20 minutes in the hot oven, until the cheese is melted and golden.

14
'Sunday Lunch'
Dishes

This chapter shows simply and clearly how to cook the traditional Sunday lunch: how to roast beef, chicken, lamb and pork. For those who don't eat meat, I've included a recipe for a Nut Roast. At the end of the chapter, there are also recipes on how to make gravy and all the other different sauces that accompany the various meats. All the traditional 'Sunday Lunch' recipes are for several people – according to the size of joint you buy – which is useful when you have weekend visitors.

ROAST BEEF
It is best if several people can share a joint, as a very small

joint is not an economical buy, for it tends to shrink up during cooking. Therefore you get better value with a larger joint which should turn out moist and delicious.

JOINTS TO CHOOSE FOR ROASTING:
Topside
Lean.

Sirloin
Delicious, but it does have a fair amount of fat around the lean meat.

Rolled Rib
May be a little cheaper than sirloin.

Choose a joint of beef that looks appetising with clear bright red lean meat and firm pale-cream fat. A good joint must have a little fat with it, or it will be too dry when roasted.

Make sure you know the weight of the joint you buy, as cooking time depends on the weight. *You should allow approximately 6 oz (175g) uncooked weight of beef per person*, so a joint weighing 2½–3 lb (1–1.5kg) should provide 6 to 8 helpings (remember you can save some cold meat for dinner next day). For underdone 'rare' beef allow 15 minutes per lb (450g) plus an extra 15 minutes. For medium-done beef allow 20 minutes per lb (450g) plus an extra 20 minutes. Remember that a small joint will cook through quicker, as it is not so thick as a big joint, so allow slightly less time.

Serve beef with Yorkshire pudding, horseradish sauce, gravy, roast potatoes and assorted vegetables or a green salad.

Place the joint in a greased roasting tin, with a little lard, dripping, margarine or oil on top. The joint, or the whole tin, may be covered with foil, to help keep the meat moist. Roast in a hot oven (400°F/200°C/Gas Mark 6–7) for the appropriate time (as explained above). Test that the meat is cooked by stabbing it with a fork or vegetable knife, and note the colour of the juices that run out: the redder the juice the more rare the meat. When the meat is cooked, lift it out carefully onto a hot plate and make the gravy (see page 230).

For the roast potatoes: calculate when the joint will be ready and allow the potatoes 45 to 60 minutes roasting time, according to size. They can be roasted around the joint, or in a separate tin in the oven. (See page 108.)

YORKSHIRE PUDDING

Individual Yorkshire puddings are baked in patty (bun) tins, but a larger pudding can be cooked in any baking tin (not one with a loose base!), but they do not cook very well in a pyrex-type dish.

Preparation and cooking time: 25 minutes (small)
40–45 minutes (large).

4 heaped tbsp PLAIN flour
Pinch of salt
1 egg
2 cups (½ pt/300ml) milk
Little oil or fat

Put the flour and salt in a basin (use a clean saucepan if you do not have a large basin). Add the egg and beat into the flour, gradually adding the milk, and beating to make a smooth batter. (The easiest way of doing this is with a hand or electric mixer, but with a bit more effort you get just as good a result using a whisk, a wooden spoon or even a fork.) Beat well.

Put the tins, with the fat in, on the top shelf of the oven (400°F/200°C/Gas Mark 6–7) for a few minutes to get hot. Give the batter a final whisk, and pour it into the tins. Bake until firm and golden brown. Try not to open the oven door for the first 10 minutes so that the puds rise well. If you want meat and puds ready together, start cooking the puds 25 minutes before the meat is ready for small puds, 40–45 minutes before for large puds.

222

ROAST CHICKEN

It may sound odd, but larger chickens are far more economical: you get more meat and less bone for your money, so it's worth sharing a chicken between several people, and keeping some cold for the next day (keep it in the fridge and don't keep it too long). The scrappy bits left on the carcass can be chopped up and used to make a risotto.

Before cooking a frozen chicken, make sure the chicken is completely defrosted by leaving it out at room temperature for several hours according to the instructions on the wrapper. It can be soaked in cold (not hot) water to get rid of the last bits of ice and hurry the thawing process but do not try to thaw it in hot water as the chicken will be tough when cooked. (See page 183.)

A 2–2½ lb (900–1100g) chicken will serve 2 to 3 people, while a 3–4 lb (1350–1800g) chicken will serve 4 to 6 people, according to appetite. Make sure you know the weight of the bird as cooking time depends on the weight. Allow 20 minutes per lb (450g) plus 20 minutes extra. Very small chickens (2–2½ lb/900–1100g) may only need 15 minutes per lb (450g) plus 15 minutes extra.

Chicken is traditionally served with chipolata sausages, thyme and parsley stuffing and bread sauce. We like apple sauce or cranberry sauce with it as well. Roast potatoes, parsnips, carrots and sprouts are tasty with chicken in the winter, while new potatoes and peas make a good summer dinner.

1 chicken (completely defrosted)
Small potato (optional)
Oil and butter (for roasting)
Cooking foil

Heat the oven (400°F/200°C/Gas Mark 6–7). Rinse the chicken in cold water and dry with kitchen paper. It is now thought best to roast chicken without putting stuffing inside. The stuffing sometimes causes the meat not to be thoroughly cooked. If you are making stuffing, cook it separately in a

223

greased dish, according to the instructions on the packet (see page 235), or only put a little inside the chicken. I sometimes put a small, peeled raw potato inside the chicken as the steam from the potato keeps the chicken moist.

Spread the butter and oil liberally over the chicken (you can cover the breast and legs with butter papers if you have any) and either wrap the chicken loosely in foil and put it into a tin, or put it into a greased roasting tin and cover the tin with foil. Put the chicken in the tin into the hot oven. Calculate the cooking time so that the rest of the dinner is ready at the same time.

Sausages, roast potatoes and parsnips can be cooked round the chicken or in a separate roasting tin. Sausages will take 20 to 30 minutes; potatoes and parsnips about 45 minutes to 1 hour.

Remove or open the foil for the last 15 minutes of cooking time, to brown the chicken. Test that the chicken is cooked by prodding it with a pointed knife or fork in the thickest part, inside the thigh. The juices should run clear; if they are still pink, cook for a little longer. Remove the chicken carefully onto a hot plate, and use the juices in the tin to make the gravy. (See page 230.)

ROAST LAMB

Leg and shoulder are both expensive joints. Shoulder is cheaper than leg, but tends to be more fatty. These joints are usually sold on the bone, so you have to allow more weight of meat for each person than you do with beef. However, trying to carve a shoulder of lamb can provide quite an entertaining cabaret act! *Allow at least 8 oz (225g) per serving*; so a joint weighing 2¼–2½ lb (about 1kg) should serve 4 people adequately.

Stuffed breast of lamb is a far more economical joint and makes a cheap Sunday dinner. A large breast of lamb will serve at least 2 generous helpings. The traditional accompaniments for lamb are mint sauce, mint jelly, redcurrant jelly or onion sauce. Serve with roast potatoes, parsnips or other vegetables.

ROAST LEG OR SHOULDER OF LAMB

You don't have to buy a whole leg or shoulder; half legs and shoulders, or a piece of a very large joint can be bought. Make sure you know the weight of the meat you buy as cooking time depends on the weight. *Allow 20 minutes per lb (450g) plus an extra 20 minutes.*

Joint of leg or shoulder of lamb
Oil or dripping (for roasting)
2–3 cloves of garlic (optional)
2–3 sprigs of rosemary (optional)

Heat the oven (400°F/200°C/Gas Mark 6–7). Place the joint in a roasting tin, with a little oil or dripping. If you like the flavour of garlic, you can insert 1 or 2 peeled cloves under the skin of the meat, near the bone, to impart a garlic flavour to the meat, but lamb has a lovely flavour so this is not really necessary. Rosemary sprigs can be used in the same way.

Cover the joint, or the whole tin, with cooking foil. (This helps to stop the meat shrivelling up.) Roast it in the hot oven for the calculated time, removing the foil for the last 20 to 30 minutes of the cooking time, to brown the meat, if it is a bit pale under the foil. Roast potatoes and parsnips can be cooked with the joint for the last hour of cooking time.

Test that the lamb is cooked at the end of the cooking time by stabbing it with a fork or vegetable knife. Lamb is traditionally served pink in the middle, but many people prefer it cooked more; it is entirely a matter of personal preference. The meat juices should run slightly tinged with pink for underdone lamb, and clear when the lamb is better cooked. When the meat is cooked satisfactorily, lift it carefully onto a hot plate and make the gravy. Serve with mint sauce.

ROAST STUFFED BREAST OF LAMB

An extremely economical roast. A large breast of lamb will serve 2 people and makes a very cheap roast dinner. Try to buy boned meat or ask the butcher to bone it for you. If you purchase one with the bones in, it is fairly easy to remove them yourself with a sharp knife, but be careful not to bone your fingers at the same time!

Serve with gravy, mint sauce, roast potatoes and parsnips, or other vegetables.

Preparation and cooking time: 1 hour 40 minutes – 2 hours 10 minutes.

1 packet (3 oz/75g size) thyme and parsley stuffing
Juice of ½ lemon (optional)
1 large breast (2 lb/900g approx.) of lamb (boned if possible)
½ yard (0.5 metre) clean string or 6 wooden cocktail sticks or toothpicks
1 tbsp oil (for cooking)
Piece of cooking foil

Heat the oven (350°F/180°C/Gas Mark 4–5). Make the stuffing as directed on the packet, adding lemon juice to the hot water before mixing the stuffing to give a tangy flavour.

Spread the stuffing over the lamb, and roll it up carefully, not too tightly. Tie it up in 2 or 3 places with the string, or secure in a roll with cocktail sticks. Lightly rub the outside of the meat with the oil, and either wrap the meat in the foil and place it in a roasting tin, or put the meat in a greased roasting tin and cover the tin with the foil.

Cook in the oven for 1½ to 2 hours, according to the size of the joint (a bigger joint will take longer) unwrapping or removing the foil for the last half hour of the cooking time to brown the meat.

ROAST PORK

Most pork joints are sold with the bone in, so you have to allow more weight of meat per serving to make up for this. (It also makes it more difficult to carve.)

Joints to choose for roasting:
Leg: the leanest and most expensive.
Shoulder: cheaper and just as tasty.
Loin: chops, left in one piece, not cut up.

Allow about 8 oz (250g) per serving; a 2½–3 lb (1125–1350g) joint should serve 4 to 6 people. Make sure you know the weight of your joint, as cooking time depends on the weight. *Allow 25 minutes per lb (450g) plus 25 minutes extra.*

Pork is traditionally served with sage and onion stuffing, and apple sauce. Also serve it with roast potatoes and parsnips or other vegetables.

Heat the oven (400°F/200°C/Gas Mark 6–7) so that the joint goes into a hot oven, to make the crackling crisp. Rub the pork skin with oil, and sprinkle with salt to give the cracking a good flavour. Place the joint in the roasting tin with a little oil or fat to stop it sticking to the tin. Put the tin into the hot oven and calculate the cooking time so that the rest of the dinner can be ready at the right time.

After 20 minutes or so, when the crackling is looking crisp, the joint or the whole tin can be covered with foil to stop the meat getting too brown (smaller joints will brown more easily). Roast potatoes or parsnips can be cooked around the meat for the last hour of the cooking time, or in a separate roasting tin. Cook the stuffing in a greased dish, according to the instructions on the packet (see page 235).

Test that the meat is cooked at the end of the cooking time: the juices should run clear when prodded with a knife or fork. If they are still pink, cook for a bit longer. Pork must be cooked right through (it is better overcooked than underdone) as rare pork can cause food poisoning. The meat should be pale-coloured, not pink. When it is completely cooked, lift it onto a hot plate and make the gravy.

NUT ROAST
Serves 2

The traditional vegetarian 'Sunday Lunch' meal that everyone has heard of. This recipe makes enough for two portions since cold nut roast is tasty too. If you have a freezer, the second portion can be frozen, uncooked, for use later. Serve with tomato sauce.

Preparation and cooking time: 45 minutes (individual dishes)
60 minutes (larger dishes).

1 onion
1 stick of celery
4 oz (100g/1 very full cup) mixed nuts, roughly chopped (a processor or liquidiser is useful for this)
2 large fresh tomatoes or use the tomatoes from a small (7 oz/ 230g) can of tomatoes (you can use the juice as an aperitif)
1 tbsp oil and a knob of butter (for frying)
3 oz (75g/3 full cups) fresh wholemeal breadcrumbs
Salt and pepper
½ tsp mixed herbs
Pinch of chilli powder
1 egg
Piece of foil (for covering the dishes)

Grease two individual dishes or one larger tin (foil dishes are useful for this). Heat the oven to 400°F/200°C/Gas Mark 6–7.

Peel and chop the onion. Wash and chop the celery. Chop the nuts. Chop the tomatoes.

Heat the oil and butter in a large frying pan or saucepan over a moderate heat and fry the onion and celery gently for 4 to 5 minutes until softened but not browned. Remove from the heat. Add the nuts, breadcrumbs, chopped tomatoes, salt, pepper, herbs and chilli powder.

Beat the egg in a small basin or cup and stir into the mixture. Taste, and adjust the seasoning and herbs if necessary.

Spoon into the well-greased tins and cover lightly with greased cooking foil. Bake in the hot oven as follows: small tins – 20 to 30 minutes, removing the foil after 15 minutes; large tins – 45 to 60 minutes, removing the foil after 30 minutes.

GRAVY

Often the meat juices alone from grilled or fried meat make a tasty sauce poured over the meat. But if you want to make 'real' gravy remember the more flour you use the thicker the gravy. The liquid can be any mixture of water, vegetable water, wine, sherry, beer or cider.

Preparation and cooking time: 4 minutes.

1–2 tsp cornflour or flour and 1 tsp gravy flavouring powder or 2 tsp gravy granules
1 cup (¼ pt/150ml) water or vegetable water and/or wine, beer, sherry, cider
Any juices from the meat

Mix the cornflour or flour and the gravy flavouring powder (if used) into a smooth paste with a little of the cold water, wine, cider, sherry or even beer (depending on what you're drinking). Add the rest of the water and the meat juices from the roasting tin.

Pour the mixture into a small saucepan, and bring to the boil, stirring all the time. Stir gravy granules, if used, straight into the hot liquid. Add more liquid if the gravy is too thick, or more flour mixture if it is too thin.

To thicken the gravy used in stews and casseroles, make the gravy mixture as above. Stir the mixture into the stew or casserole and bring to the boil so that the gravy can thicken as it cooks.

WHITE SAUCE

This is a quick way to make a basic sauce, to which you can add other ingredients or flavourings.

Preparation and cooking time: 5 minutes.

2 tsp cornflour (or flour)
1 cup (¼ pt/150ml) milk
½ oz (12g) butter (or margarine)
Salt and pepper

Put the cornflour or flour in a large cup or small basin. Mix it into a runny paste with 1 tbsp of the milk. Boil the rest of the milk in a saucepan. Pour it onto the well-stirred flour mixture, stirring all the time. Pour the mixture back into the saucepan, return to the heat and bring to the boil, stirring all the time, until the sauce thickens. Beat in the butter or margarine. Season with the salt and pepper.

CHEESE SAUCE
Grate 1–2 oz (25–50g) cheese. Add to the white sauce with the butter, and add a dash of mustard if you have any.

PARSLEY SAUCE
Wash and drain a handful of sprigs of parsley. Chop them finely with a knife or scissors, and add to the sauce with the salt and pepper.

ONION SAUCE

A quick and easy method. Onion sauce is traditionally served with lamb, and is also tasty poured over cauliflower.

Preparation and cooking time: 25 minutes.

1 onion
1 cup (¼ pt/150ml) water
2 tsp flour or cornflour
1 cup (¼ pt/150ml) milk
Knob of butter
Salt and pepper

Peel and finely chop the onion. Put it into a small saucepan, with the cup of water. Bring to the boil, then lower the heat and cook gently for 10 to 15 minutes, until the onion is soft.

In a bowl mix the flour or cornflour into a paste with a little of the milk. Gradually add this to the onion mixture, stirring all the time as the mixture thickens. Add more milk, until the sauce is just thick enough – not runny, but not like blancmange. Beat in the knob of butter, and season with the salt and pepper. Serve hot.

'INSTANT' SAUCE MIX

Several makes of sauce mix are now widely available at supermarkets. Follow the instructions on the packet, and only make up as much sauce as is needed for the recipe. Keep the rest of the packet for later, tightly closed, in a dry cupboard or fridge.

BREAD SAUCE

Serve it with chicken. I generally use a packet of bread sauce mix, which is very easy to make, cooks quickly and tastes good, especially with the addition of a little extra butter and a spoonful of cream. Allow 1 cup (¼ pt) milk for 1 to 2 servings; 2 cups (½ pt) milk will make enough sauce for 2 to 4 people, according to your appetites.

1 packet bread sauce mix (you may only need to use part of the packet, but the rest will keep in the store cupboard)
1 cup (¼ pt/150ml) milk
Knob of butter (¼ oz/8g) – optional
2 tsp cream – optional

Make the sauce according to the instructions on the packet. Stir in the butter and cream just before serving. Left-over sauce will keep overnight in the fridge and can be used on cold chicken sandwiches.

APPLE SAUCE

You can buy jars or tins of apple purée, but it is cheaper and very easy to make your own. Apple sauce is served with roast pork or poultry.

Preparation and cooking time: 10–15 minutes.

1–2 cooking apples
2–3 tbsp water
1–2 tbsp sugar

Peel, core and slice the apples. Put them in a saucepan with the water and bring to the boil gently. Simmer for 5 to 10 minutes, until the apples are soft (do not let them boil dry). Add the sugar to taste (be careful, the apples will be *very* hot) and mash with a fork until smooth.

MINT SAUCE

You can buy jars of mint sauce at the supermarket, but I think they taste better if you re-mix the sauce with a little sugar and 1 to 2 teaspoons of fresh vinegar. Mint sauce is traditionally served with lamb.

'BOUGHT' MINT SAUCE

3–4 tsp 'bought' mint sauce
1 tsp granulated sugar
1–2 tsp vinegar

Mix all the above ingredients together in a small glass or dish.

'FRESH' MINT SAUCE

Handful of fresh mint sprigs
2–3 tbsp vinegar (wine vinegar if you have it)
1–2 tsp granulated sugar

Strip the leaves from the stems. Wash well, drain and chop the mint as finely as possible. Mix the mint, vinegar and sugar in a small glass or dish, and serve with the lamb. This sauce will keep in a small, covered jar in the fridge.

STUFFING

Traditionally, sage and onion stuffing goes with pork, while thyme and parsley goes with chicken, but any mixture of herbs is tasty.

Preparation and cooking time: 35–45 minutes.

1 packet (3 oz/75g size) stuffing
A little butter or margarine
Hot water – you can use water from the kettle or vegetable water

Make up the stuffing according to the directions on the packet. Grease an oven-proof dish, put the stuffing into the dish, dot with the butter. Bake in the oven (400°F/200°C/Gas Mark 6–7) with the joint, for 30 to 40 minutes, until crispy on top.

15
Puddings and Cakes

A few easy recipes for those with a sweet tooth.

Lots of delicious chilled and frozen desserts, gooey gateaux and sticky buns are widely available ready-made in the shops and can provide an instant treat.

Scan the packets of cake, pudding and biscuit mixes on the supermarket shelves. With the addition of butter and eggs, you can easily produce a home-made cake.

QUICK CHOCOLATE SAUCE – FOR ICE-CREAM
Serves 1

Fast, easy and most effective. It has a lovely, chocolatey flavour but is not too rich.

Preparation and cooking time: 5 minutes.

1 chocolate bar (1–2 oz/25–50g size)
1 tsp cold water

Break the chocolate into a pottery or pyrex basin or jug, with
1 tsp of water. Stand the basin in 1 in (2.5cm) hot water in a
saucepan over a low heat, and simmer gently until the
chocolate melts. Stir well, and pour the chocolate sauce over
scoops of ice-cream.

HOT CHOCOLATE SAUCE – SERVE WITH ICE-CREAM
Serves 1

A rich fudgy sauce, delicious with vanilla, chocolate or
coffee-flavoured ice-cream.

Preparation and cooking time: 10 minutes.

**2 oz (50g) chocolate chips, chocolate cake covering or a
    chocolate bar**
1 tbsp brown sugar
1 tbsp cold water
1 oz (25g) butter (unsalted is best)
2 tsp rum (optional)

Put the chocolate, sugar and water into a small saucepan,
over a low heat, and stir until the chocolate melts and the
mixture is smooth and creamy. Remove from the heat. Add
the butter in small flakes. Beat well. Beat in the rum, if used.
Serve, poured over scoops of ice-cream. If necessary, re-heat
the sauce later by putting it into a pyrex or pottery basin or
jug, and stand this in 1 in (2.5cm) hot water in a saucepan.
Put the saucepan over a low heat and simmer gently until the
sauce melts again, stirring well.

BANANA SPLIT

Serves 1

Full of calories, but absolutely delicious!

Preparation time: 5 minutes (plus the time for making the chocolate sauce).

1 large banana
2–3 tbsp ice-cream
1 tbsp chocolate sauce (bought or home-made – see page 237)
1 tbsp thick cream – spooning cream is ideal
Chopped nuts (for decoration – optional)
Chocolate sprinkles (for decoration – optional)

Split the banana in half, lengthways, then place it on a plate. Sandwich the banana halves together with spoonfuls of ice-cream. Spoon the chocolate sauce over the top. Decorate with the cream and sprinkle nuts or chocolate sprinkles on the top. Eat immediately.

FRUIT PAVLOVA

Serves 1

A super summer sweet. Make it with cream, ice-cream – or both!

Preparation time: 5 minutes.

1–2 tbsp fresh or canned fruit – raspberries, strawberries, canned peaches, mandarins, pineapples, pears
1–2 tbsp thick cream (spooning cream is good) and/or 1–2 tbsp ice-cream
1–2 meringue nests (available in packets from supermarkets)

Prepare this dish just before you are ready to eat it. Wash and drain the fresh fruit, or drain the canned fruit. Spread the ice-cream over the meringue nests. Arrange the fresh or canned fruit carefully on top of the cream or ice-cream. Decorate with a spoonful of thick cream. Serve at once.

SPONGE FRUIT FLAN   *Serves 2*

So easy, yet looks most impressive. Choose fruit and jelly whose flavours complement each other.

Preparation and cooking time: 10 minutes (plus setting time).

½ tin (15½ oz/439g size) fruit in natural juice or syrup (oranges, peaches, pineapples, pears, etc.)
Water if necessary
1 packet (1 pt size) jelly – any flavour
A 6 in/15cm sponge flan case or 2 individual flan cases (available from large supermarkets)

Open the tin of fruit and strain the juice or syrup into a cup. Make up ½ pint (2 cupfuls) of the fruit juice by adding water if necessary. Heat the juice and water in a saucepan, until it is just boiling. Remove from the heat and add the jelly. Stir until the jelly melts. Leave a few minutes to cool, then put into the fridge, freezer or other cold place, until the jelly is half-set. (This will take about ½ to 1 hour according to the temperature; the colder it is, the quicker the jelly will set.)

When the jelly is half-set, arrange the fruit in the sponge flan in pretty patterns. Spoon the half-set jelly on the top and leave in a cool place to set completely (15–30 minutes, depending on the temperature). Leave any spare jelly to set, then mash with a fork and serve separately with any spare fruit. (If the jelly gets too set before you remember to finish the flan, it can be thinned down by carefully adding 1 to 2 tbsp boiling water to the set jelly and stirring hard, to make it soft again.)

CRUNCHY CREAM PIE

Serves 2–3

Easy to make, and delicious served with cream or ice-cream. You can use any flavour of instant flavoured milk dessert for the filling – chocolate or butterscotch are lovely.

Preparation time: 15 minutes.

3–4 oz (75–100g) plain digestive biscuits
2 oz (50g) butter or block margarine
2 heaped tbsp brown sugar (use white if you haven't any brown)
1 packet instant flavoured milk dessert
2 cups (½ pt/300ml) milk

Put the biscuits into a deep bowl or a clean polythene bag and crush them into crumbs with a rolling pin or wooden spoon. Melt the butter in a saucepan over a very low heat (do not let it brown or burn), then stir in the sugar and biscuit crumbs and mix well. Press this mixture into a greased deep pie plate, pie dish or baking tin (6–7 in/15–18cm in diameter), spreading it round to make a flan case (there is no cooking, so it does not have to be an oven-proof dish).

Put the flan in a cold place to cool. Make up the instant flavoured milk dessert with the milk as instructed on the packet. Whisk with a whisk, mixer or fork. Leave for a minute so that it partly sets. Pour into the biscuit crust and smooth the top. Leave it in a cool place or fridge for a few minutes to set.

PANCAKES

Makes 6–8 pancakes

These can be sweet or savoury, and are delicious any day, not just on Shrove Tuesday (Pancake Day). Sweet pancakes are traditionally served sprinkled with 1 tsp sugar and a squeeze of lemon. For sweet and savoury fillings see page 31.

Preparation time: 10 minutes (plus 1 minute per pancake cooking time).

4 heaped tbsp (4 oz/100g) plain flour
1 egg
2 cups (½ pt/300ml) milk
Oil or lard for frying – not butter

Prepare the filling if used. Put the flour into a bowl (use a medium-sized saucepan if you don't have one). Add the egg, and beat it into the flour. Gradually add the milk and beat to make a smooth batter (the easiest way of doing this is with a hand or electric mixer, but with a bit of effort you get just as good a result using a wooden spoon or even a fork).

Heat a clean frying pan over a moderate heat, and when hot, but not burning, grease the pan with a smear of oil or lard (approximately ½ tsp). Pour in a little batter, enough to cover the pan thinly. Tilt the pan to spread the batter over it. Fry briskly, until just set on top, and lightly browned underneath, shaking the pan occasionally to stop the pancake sticking – this will only take a few moments.

Toss the pancake, or flip it over with a knife, and fry for a few more moments to cook the other side. Turn it out onto a warm plate. Sprinkle with lemon and sugar, or add the filling, and roll up or fold into four.

Pancakes taste best eaten at once, straight from the pan, but they can be filled, rolled up and kept warm while you cook the rest. Wipe the pan with a pad of kitchen paper, re-heat and re-grease the pan, and cook the next pancake as before.

SYRUPY PEACHES

Serves 1

Make this lovely pudding when fresh peaches are cheap in the greengrocer's. Serve hot with cream or ice-cream. (This dish can be prepared, but not cooked, in advance, the cold fruit being left to soak in the syrup, and then put in the oven to cook while you are eating your first course.)

Preparation and cooking time: 15 minutes.

2 tbsp brown sugar
½ cup water
1–2 peaches

Make the syrup: put the brown sugar and water into a small saucepan, bring to the boil, stirring occasionally, and simmer gently for 3 to 4 minutes to dissolve the sugar. Wash the peaches (do not peel) and cut them in half, from top to bottom. Remove the stones. Put the peaches into an oven-proof dish with the cut sides face upwards, and pour the hot syrup over the fruit, spooning it into the holes left by the stones. Put into a warm oven (350°F/180°C/Gas Mark 4), for 10 to 15 minutes, until the fruit is hot and the syrup bubbling.

GRILLED PEACHES

Serves 1

Absolutely delicious with fresh peaches, but very good with tinned fruit too. Buy cheap peaches in the summer for a treat. Serve with cream or ice-cream.

Preparation and cooking time: 5 minutes.

1–2 fresh peaches or ½ a tin (15oz/425g size) of peaches
1 oz (25g) butter
2 tbsp demerara sugar

Peel and slice the fresh peaches or drain and slice the tinned peaches. Butter an oven-proof dish, and place the peach slices in the dish. Sprinkle thickly with the brown sugar, dot with some butter. Place the dish under a hot grill for a minute or two, so that the sugar melts and the peach slices warm through. Serve at once.

LIQUEUR ORANGES

Serves 2

Delicious, simple and rather unusual, so save it for when you are entertaining a special friend.

Preparation time: 5 minutes.
Chilling time: 1–2 hours, but longer if possible; all day is best.

2 large, sweet oranges
2 tbsp sugar
1 tbsp orange liqueur – Cointreau, Grand Marnier or Curaçao (you can buy a miniature bottle of liqueur)
Thick cream (optional)

Peel the oranges and scrape away any white pith. Cut the oranges into thin rings, and arrange the slices in a shallow serving dish. Sprinkle with the sugar and liqueur. Cover the dish with a plate or cling film and leave it in the fridge or in a cold place for at least an hour, but all day if possible, to chill and let the liqueur soak in. Serve alone or with thick cream.

BREAD 'PUDDEN'

Serves 2–3

A good way of using up stale bread, very quick to prepare but do allow time for the bread to soak. Serve hot or cold, on its own, or with cream or custard.

Preparation and cooking time: 45 minutes
plus 20 minutes soaking.

4 oz (100g) stale bread – brown, white or a mixture
1 cup (¼ pt/150ml) milk
2–3 oz (50–75g) mixed dried fruit
2 oz (50g) sugar
2 oz (50g) butter (it's nicer than margarine)
1 small or approx. ½ egg
1 tsp mixed spice
Pinch of grated nutmeg

Break the bread into small pieces, put into a mixing bowl and cover with the milk. Stir well and leave to soak for about 30 minutes until the bread has soaked up the milk.

Heat the oven to 350°F/180°C/Gas Mark 4–5. Grease a 1½ pt (1 litre) oven-proof pie dish well.

Wash and drain the dried fruit and stir it into the soaked bread and milk, with the sugar and the butter chopped into little pieces. Beat the egg in a small basin with the spice and stir into the pudding, mixing well. Pour the mixture into the greased dish, and sprinkle with a little more grated nutmeg. Bake in the moderate oven for 25 to 30 minutes until set.

BREAD AND BUTTER PUDDING

Serves 2

This is great for using up those slices of bread going stale in the fridge. The recipe makes a delicious tasty pud with a crispy top (I leave the crusts on for extra crunch). With all the eggs and milk in the recipe, it makes a good dish to serve after a lighter or vegetarian first course. It can also make a good supper dish – much more interesting than poached egg on toast with a glass of milk! Serve hot, on its own or with thick cream.

Preparation and cooking time: 45 minutes
plus 20 minutes soaking.

3 slices of bread (large loaf)
2 oz (50g) butter (nicer than margarine), softened
2 oz (50g) currants or sultanas
1 oz (25g) sugar
1 egg
½ pt (0.25 litre) milk
¼ tsp vanilla essence

Grease a 1½ pt (1 litre) deep pie or oven-proof dish well. Remove the crusts from the bread if you wish, and butter the bread. Cut the slices into triangles and arrange a layer of bread on the base of the dish, butter side down. Sprinkle this with half of the washed drained currants or sultanas and with a tbsp of sugar. Cover with another layer of bread, sprinkle with the rest of the fruit and another tbsp of sugar. Top with the rest of the bread, butter side up, and sprinkle with the remaining sugar.

Beat the eggs, mix in the milk and essence and pour over the pud. Leave to soak for about 30 minutes, or longer, until the bread has nearly soaked up all the milk.

Heat the oven to 325°F/170°C/Gas Mark 3–4. Bake the pud in the moderate oven for 25 to 30 minutes until set with a lovely golden crispy top.

POOR KNIGHTS' PUDDING   *Serves 2*

Those knights knew a thing or two – maybe they made this at
the end of the week when the king was a bit late with the
wage cheques! It may be cheap but it's delicious and filling; a
sophisticated version of the boarding school favourite, eggy
bread.

Use up any kind of bread – brown, white or leftover jam or
honey sandwiches – or make the French *pain perdu*, using
rounds of French bread. The knights undoubtedly used
dripping or lard for frying, but a mixture of oil and butter will
please the health-conscious modern taste.

Preparation and cooking time: 20 minutes.

**2–6 thick slices of bread (brown, white or French), according
   to size, or 4–8 jam or honey sandwiches**
1 egg, plus an extra yolk if it's spare
1 cup (¼ pt/150ml) milk
½ glass sherry or brandy (optional)
2–3 tsp sugar, to taste
3–4 tbsp oil with 1 oz (25g) butter (for frying)

Topping:
**1–2 tbsp sugar, left plain or mixed with 1 tsp cinnamon,
   nutmeg or mixed spice, as preferred**

Cut the crusts off the bread and discard. Cut the bread into
dainty sandwich-sized triangles or squares, or make small
jam or honey sandwiches and put into a shallow dish.

Put the egg, and extra yolk if used, into a basin and beat
well, beating in the milk, sherry or brandy, and sugar to
taste. Pour the egg mixture over the bread and leave for a
few minutes to soak. Turn the bread over carefully and leave
for a few more minutes until all the egg is soaked into the
bread.

Heat the oil and butter in a large frying pan over a
moderate heat until just hazing, and, using a fish slice,
carefully put the soaked bread slices into the hot fat. Cook

for a few moments until golden, then turn and cook the other side. Drain on kitchen paper and serve on a warm plate, dredged with the prepared sugar.

PEANUT CRUNCH
A crunchy cake to eat with coffee.

Preparation time: 10 minutes (plus setting time).

1 packet (7–8 oz/200–225g) plain digestive, rich tea or other plain biscuits
2 oz (50g) butter or block margarine
2 tbsp brown sugar (white will do)
4 tbsp golden syrup or honey
4 tbsp crunchy peanut butter

Grease a square or round shallow tin (approximately 7 in (17.5cm) in diameter). Put the biscuits in a deep bowl or a polythene bag and crush them not too finely with a rolling pin or wooden spoon. Melt the butter, sugar and syrup in a saucepan over a low heat, stirring well, until the butter is melted and the sugar has dissolved. Remove from the heat, and stir in the peanut butter. Mix in the biscuits, stir well. Press into the greased tin, and leave in the fridge or a cool place until set (½–1 hour according to temperature). Cut into squares or fingers.

CHOCOLATE CRUNCHIES

This has to be the easiest cake recipe there is, anywhere.

Preparation and cooking time: 5 minutes.

4 oz (100g) chocolate cake covering, cooking chocolate or chocolate bar
2 cups (2 oz/50g) cornflakes or rice crispies
12–15 paper cases

Break the chocolate into a pyrex or pottery basin. Stand this in 1 in (2.5cm) of hot water in a saucepan. Simmer this over a gentle heat until the chocolate melts. Remove the basin from the pan (use a cloth, the basin will be hot) and stir in the cornflakes or crispies, and mix until they are well-coated with the chocolate. Spoon into heaps in the paper cases, and leave to set. Store in a tin or plastic box.

CHOCOLATE KRISPIES

Almost everyone likes these, and they're cheap too. Instead of the sugar and cocoa you can use 4 tbsp drinking chocolate.

Preparation and cooking time: 15 minutes.

2 oz (50g) butter or block margarine
2 tbsp sugar
2 tbsp golden syrup
2 tbsp (level) cocoa
3 cups (3 oz/75g) cornflakes or rice crispies
12–15 paper cases

Put the butter (or margarine), sugar and syrup in a medium-sized saucepan, and heat over a gentle heat until melted. Stir in the cocoa (or drinking chocolate) and stir well to make a chocolate syrup. Stir in the cornflakes or crispies, and mix well to coat them thoroughly. Heap them into the paper cases and leave to set. Store in a tin or plastic box.

CHOCOLATE BISCUIT CAKE

This can be made in any shape of shallow baking tin or dish. It does not need baking, just leave it to cool, then cover with melted chocolate and cut into squares.

Preparation and cooking time: 20 minutes (plus setting time).

1 packet (7–8 oz/200–225g) plain digestive or rich tea biscuits
4 oz (100g) butter or block margarine
2 tsp sugar
2 tsp cocoa or 4 tsp drinking chocolate
1 tbsp golden syrup or honey
½ packet (4 oz/100g) chocolate cake covering (you can use cooking chocolate or chocolate bars)

Grease a square or round shallow sandwich cake baking tin (approximately 7–8 in/17.5–20cm in diameter). Crush the biscuits (not too finely) by putting them into a deep bowl or a clean polythene bag, and crushing them with a rolling pin or wooden spoon.

Put the butter, sugar, cocoa and syrup into a medium-sized saucepan, and melt slowly over a low heat, stirring occasionally. Remove from the heat. Add the crushed biscuits and mix well. Press into the prepared tin, spread flat and leave to cool (10 to 15 minutes).

Melt the chocolate by breaking it into a pyrex or pottery basin or jug and standing this in 1 in (2.5cm) hot water in a saucepan over a low heat. Simmer gently until the chocolate melts. Pour the chocolate over the biscuit cake, spread evenly and leave to set for 15–30 minutes in a cool place. Cut into squares or fingers and store in a tin or plastic box.

DROP SCONES OR SCOTCH PANCAKES

Fun to make for tea on a cold weekend afternoon.

Preparation and cooking time: 20 minutes.

4 heaped tbsp self-raising flour
   **or 4 heaped tbsp plain flour and 1 tsp cream of tartar and
   ½ tsp bicarbonate of soda**
1 egg
1 cup (¼ pt/150ml) milk
Little oil or lard (not butter) for greasing
Clean tea-towel or napkin

Put the flour (and cream of tartar and bicarbonate of soda if using plain flour) into a bowl. (Use a medium-sized saucepan if you don't have a bowl.) Add the egg, and beat it into the flour, gradually adding the milk and beating to make a smooth batter. (Use a hand or electric mixer if you have one, but you get just as good a result using a wooden spoon or a fork.) The batter will be much thicker than pancake or Yorkshire Pudding batter.

Heat a clean frying pan, or a griddle (a flat iron pan for baking cakes), over a moderate heat. When it is quite hot, but not burning, grease it lightly with the oil or lard, and drop one tablespoon of the batter at a time onto the pan. Drop the tablespoonfuls so that they fall far enough apart from each other to allow room for each of them to spread slightly. You can probably cook 3 or 4 pancakes at a time. Cook for 1½ to 2 minutes, until there are little bubbles on the top of the pancakes and the underneath is light brown. Turn them over gently with a knife and cook the other side for a few minutes. Remove them from the pan and place them on a clean cloth, folding it over to keep the scones moist as they cool. Serve with lots of butter, jam, or clotted cream for a treat.

YUMMY BANANA BREAD

Use up any soft, ripe bananas you've got left in the fruit bowl. Eat this bread on its own or spead with butter, or, if you're really self-indulgent, with butter and apricot jam.

It's useful if you've got a food processor for this recipe; but if you haven't, you can use a wooden spoon but it will take longer and be hard work!

Preparation and cooking time: 1¼–1½ hours.

4 oz (100g) soft margarine
4 oz (100g) sugar
8 oz (225g) self-raising flour
½ tsp baking powder
Pinch of salt
2 eggs
3–4 bananas (according to size)
Grated rind of 1 orange and lemon
  or ½ tsp mixed spice
4 oz (100g) mixed dried fruit (optional)

Heat the oven to 300°F/150°C/Gas Mark 2–3. Grease a 2 lb (1kg) loaf tin well and line the base with greased greaseproof paper.

Put the margarine and sugar into a mixing bowl or processor. Sieve the flour, baking powder and salt into the bowl, add the eggs and beat well with an electric mixer, processor or wooden spoon.

Slice the bananas into a basin and mash with a fork or potato masher, then add to the cake mixture, grate in the orange or lemon rind, if used, and beat again until well mixed. Stir in the washed dried fruit and spice, if used, and mix well. Pour the mixture into the greased tin and bake in the low oven for about an hour until well risen and firm to the touch. Cool in the tin for a few minutes, then turn onto a wire tray, remove the paper and leave until cold.

Index

255